Praise for **The Brain Mechanic**

"This is heavyweight psycho-spiritual guidance doled out with a ladle of honey. Spencer is the quintessential affable guru—friendly, approachable, flexible. His 'emotional algebra' provides an invaluable formula for liberation, empowering each of us to be our own brain mechanic instead of a sniveling victim to the false self. A 'must read' for spiritual seekers—one which I will be using at Columbia College with my Mystical Consciousness students."

> **—Elizabeth-Anne Stewart, Ph.D.**,
> author and professor at Columbia College

"Concise, accessible, and indescribably powerful."

> **—David Geffen**,
> cofounder of DreamWorks SKG

"A good brain mechanic is hard to find. Usually you wind up in a chop shop. And the replacement parts are inferior. Spencer Lord has changed all that. He offers a one-stop service and you're out and running smooth before lunch. This may sound glib, but you'll feel the same way when you realize how simple it is and how stupid you were not to have realized it before you drove into that wall."

> **—Bruce Vilanch**,
> comedy writer for the Academy Awards
> and multiple Emmy winner

"Spending one night with *The Brain Mechanic* can change your life."

> **—Lori Andrews**,
> professor of law at Chicago-Kent College of Law,
> legal chair for the Human Genome Project,
> and author of *The Silent Assassin*

"A 'must-read.' I feel brighter and better having read it!"
—**Carole Bayer Sager**,
singer, painter, and Oscar- and
Emmy-winning songwriter

"Great book."

—**Sheri Salata**,
executive producer of
The Oprah Winfrey Show

"*The Brain Mechanic* empowers its readers with a simple, straightforward 'equation' for change. Perhaps EV + B = EM should be offered to all middle-school youngsters as part of the standard curriculum. How skillfully they would navigate through life learning this tool early on!"
—**Rhonda J. Noonan, M.S., L.P.C.**,
clinical director, private practitioner

"A work of preternatural genius."

—**Dr. William Cole**,
former president of Lake Forest College and
chairman of the Chicago Council on Foreign Relations

"Your brain can't run without a good mechanic. Spence is mine."

—**Howard Bragman**,
founder of Fifteen Minutes, publicist,
and author of *Where's My Fifteen Minutes?*

"Mr. Lord uses letters like words, words like thoughts, thoughts like tools, tools like dreams, and dreams like reality . . ."

—**Christopher G. Ciccone**,
artist, film director, artistic director, dancer,
interior and furniture designer, and
author of *Life with My Sister Madonna*

"Spencer Lord is a not only a mechanic of the brain but a life enlightener and surgeon of the soul."

—**Mario Cantone**,
writer, comedian, and Tony-nominated actor

"Spencer is the ultimate connector—of our friends, our dreams, and our brains."

—**Hilary Rosen**, editor-at-large,
The Huffington Post and political contributor at CNN

"Brace yourself: *The Brain Mechanic* is the best brain candy to gobble up at the moment. Spencer Lord weaves together a simple, easy-to-read guide to understanding your emotions and your behavior. More important, he provides the tools needed to create the possibility for real transformation. Delicious!"

—**Greg Archer**, *San Francisco Examiner*

"Imagine that . . . THINKING actually does play an important role in how we feel and what we do . . . *The Brain Mechanic* not only reinforces that causal link, but it arms readers with tools to apply cognitive behavioral therapy techniques in their daily lives."

—**Joe Zuniga**, president/CEO,
International Association of Physicians in AIDS Care

"Well, I thought I knew everything. Apparently not. This book has, if I say so myself, made me brilliant. I have only four words for anyone who wants to unlock the potential of his/her brain: You. Should. Read. This."

—**Elayne Boosler**, writer, comedian, and founder of Tails of Joy

"Spencer Lord has provided us with a user's manual to the human brain. By applying the material in *The Brain Mechanic*, one has the tools to positively change their life. I see this book as a step in the right direction to powerfully merge science and spirituality."

—**Jesse Brune**, founder of Project: Service L.A.,
Le Cordon Bleu–trained chef,
personal trainer, and reality television star

"It will change your outlook and your life!"

—**ANT**, comedian and VH1 host

THE BRAIN MECHANIC

THE BRAIN MECHANIC

A Quick and Easy Way to Tune Up the
Mind and Maximize Emotional Health

SPENCER LORD

Foreword by Cheryl Saban, Ph.D.

Health Communications, Inc.
Deerfield Beach, Florida

www.hcibooks.com

Library of Congress Cataloging-in-Publication Data

Lord, Spencer.
   The brain mechanic : a quick and easy way to tune up the mind
and maximize emotional health / Spencer Lord.
     p. cm.
   Includes bibliographical references and index.
   ISBN-13: 978-0-7573-1556-5
   ISBN-10: 0-7573-1556-9
   1. Cognitive therapy—Popular works.   I. Title.
RC489.C63L67 2011
616.89'1425—dc22

                                             2010039689

Publisher: Health Communications, Inc.
          3201 S.W. 15th Street
          Deerfield Beach, FL 33442–8190

Cover design by Justin Rotkowitz
Author photo by Ron Volanti
Interior design and formatting by Dawn Von Strolley Grove

For You

*"In the struggle for survival,
the fittest win out because they succeed
in adapting themselves best
to their environment."*

—CHARLES DARWIN

Contents

Foreword

The Brain Mechanic is by far the most uncomplicated and easy-to-absorb discourse on cognitive behavioral therapy I've ever read. I breezed through this little tome within hours, marking page after page with a yellow highlighter so that I could refer to it later, and most important, so I could share it with my kids and friends. I came away from reading this book with a smile on my face. It's entertaining, it makes perfect sense, it's easy to follow, and any one of us can benefit immediately from reading it.

Spencer Lord introduces the reader to several important parts of the brain, but with a slightly unorthodox methodology—he cuts to the chase and makes his material accessible to everyone. He describes the *prefrontal cortex*, the *amygdala*, and the *cingulate gyrus* in layman's terms. In other words, he takes the medical school, out-of-my-pay-scale mystery out of these important structures and turns them into neighborhood friends that we can get to know and understand.

Mr. Lord makes the argument that we can indeed control our behaviors once we understand emotional algebra. He has devised a way to teach this equation (EV + B = EM) quickly and creatively. I highly recommend *The Brain Mechanic*. I would venture to say that as you seek knowledge and actualization of mind-body wellness, self-worth, and self-esteem, emotional algebra could end up being one of the best lessons you've ever learned.

—Cheryl Saban, Ph.D.

Cheryl Saban holds a Ph.D. in psychology. She is a philanthropist and the author of *What Is Your Self-Worth? A Woman's Guide to Validation.*

Introduction

The author of this work has asked me to write an introduction to what lies ahead. As both friend and mentor, I have witnessed firsthand the many stages of Spencer Lord's personal development: his early years at the University of Chicago, his odysseys around the world and across Asia, and his work with Mother Teresa.

I have also observed his intellectual journey through successive attachments to the views of Henry Louis Mencken, Noam Chomsky, Ayn Rand, Sigmund Freud, and Richard Dawkins. In each case, there was a strong commitment, an almost adolescent "crush" on the ideas espoused.

But this latest excitement about cognitive psychology is something new. Here, there has been more than a detached agreement with ideas. The study of cognitive psychology has produced an actual transformation in Spencer's lifestyle and a degree of peace and maturity resembling that of a religious conversion.

Whereas before he was volatile, emotional, and defensive about his ideas, he now demonstrates stability, tolerance, and direction. He has shared some of his cognitive discoveries with his friends and acquaintances, and their enthusiasm and similar sense of a second birth have led him to the decision to write the pages ahead, spreading what he has found to be so enriching and fulfilling to an even wider audience.

Spencer has integrated into his life of staunch scientific skepticism a system of "faith" through brain science. He wants to share his journey and that knowledge with you and others. I believe you are going to be astonished by the simplicity and power of *The Brain Mechanic*.

Happy Reading!

—William Graham Cole, Ph.D.
Columbia University

William Cole was the president of Lake Forest College for ten years before becoming the chairman of the Chicago Council on Foreign Relations. His books include *The Restless Quest of Modern Man* (Oxford University Press) and *Sex in Christianity and Psychoanalysis* (Oxford University Press).

You are now precognitive.

Preface

Most of us know precisely what we should do. Take it easy. Have fun. Let yourself go. Don't sweat the small stuff. Roll with it. Don't let it bother you. Shake it off. Be a good sport. Chill. Be cool. Don't worry. Be happy. Relax!

That may be good advice, but I'm an intelligent individual, and I already know what I should feel and what I should do. Would anyone mind telling the less enlightened among us *how* to feel and do these things?

It took me years to finally discover a *how* that actually works, and that's when I began to share this knowledge with my friends, my family, and now you.

The cognitive model is the *how*.

You've no doubt heard the word *cognitive* countless times, and if you ever looked up the term *cognitive behavioral therapy,* you would have found something like this:

Cognitive behavioral therapy (or cognitive behavior therapies, CBT) is a psychotherapeutic approach that

5

aims to influence dysfunctional emotions, behaviors, and cognitions through a goal-oriented, systematic procedure. The title is used in diverse ways to designate behavior therapy, cognitive therapy, and to refer to therapy based upon a combination of basic behavioral and cognitive research. There is empirical evidence that CBT is effective for the treatment of a variety of problems, including mood, anxiety, personality, eating, substance abuse, and psychotic disorders.

—Wikipedia
http://en.wikipedia.org/wiki/Cognitive_behavioral_therapy

This definition sounds very fancy and scientific, but it's totally meaningless to most people. Basically, cognitive behavioral therapy demonstrates that our thoughts—not external things like people, events, or situations—cause our feelings and behaviors.

My grandmother used to tell my mother that if there was ever anything in the world she wanted to learn, she could go to the public library and figure it out. My mom passed on this advice to me, and I put it to good use. I've done the hard part for you already, by reading and distilling thousands of pages of information on psychology and human brain function. In the pages to follow, I will draw from what I learned through my research and share the most important concepts with you in an easy-to-understand way.

Cognitive behavioral therapy is not new; it has actually been around for years, but most people outside the field of psychology don't have any idea what it is or how it works. After discovering firsthand how effective these techniques are, I decided to write this book to make these concepts more accessible to the general public.

CBT can be used as a powerful survival tool, but try dragging the average survivalist in to an office full of grown-ups in neckties. Not gonna happen. So I wrote this book as a way to teach the tools of survival psychology to people who wouldn't normally go sit in an office or classroom. It's a two-hour psychological survival training course—on paper.

Since I'm an ordinary guy, not a professional writer, I hope you'll forgive the handbook's simplicity of style and tone. I'm going to talk you through these concepts just like I've taught them to my friends and family.

This book is also my personal story and testimony. I am not a doctor or a psychologist, and this book is *not* a substitute for professional mental health care. It is written for mentally and emotionally healthy individuals who want to use the tools of CBT to enrich and enhance their lives and strengthen their brains.

If you are suffering from any serious emotional problems, it is critical that you talk to your doctor immediately and seek appropriate professional care. This book is merely a layperson's introduction to cognitive psychology told through my personal journey and is in no way a substitute for psychotherapy or counseling.

If you love science and psychology as much as I do, you're in for a real treat. In the next few hours, you will have all the tools necessary to become your very own Brain Mechanic.

Hang on to your frontal lobe . . .

"The destiny of every human being
is decided by what goes on inside his
skull when confronted with
what goes on outside his skull."

—DR. ERIC BERNE

Part
One

UNDER THE HOOD:
The Cognitive Model

Simply put, the cognitive model is a functional description of how your brain works. It's like a diagram of the human thought process that helps us understand and predict how we think and feel. There are countless variations of the model as described by psychologists. And the descriptions tend to be as complicated as the models themselves! For example:

> A cognitive model is an approximation to animal cognitive processes (predominantly human) for the purposes of comprehension and prediction. Cognitive models can be developed within or without a cognitive architecture, though the two are not always easily distinguishable.
>
> In contrast to cognitive architectures, cognitive models tend to be focused on a single cognitive phenomenon or process . . . Cognitive modeling historically developed within cognitive psychology/cognitive science (including human factors) . . . There are many types of cognitive models, and they can range from box-and-arrow diagrams to a set of equations to software programs that interact with the same tools that humans use to complete tasks.
>
> —*Wikipedia*
> http://en.wikipedia.org/wiki/Cognitive_model

Don't worry if the above description doesn't make sense to you. I'll give you my description in plain English. The cognitive model that follows is my personal version. I wanted to get a jump on grad school so I started reading everything

11

I could find on the brain, psychology, psychoanalysis, and psychotherapy. Through these many months of study I was repeatedly flummoxed by how impenetrable the descriptions of various cognitive models and concepts were.

I kept wondering, *Why didn't they explain this more simply?* followed by, *I could make this so much clearer and so much easier to understand if I were teaching it, because this belongs in front of that, and you have to teach that after you teach this, and move that over there, and so on.* This book is my effort to show you the model in a way I wish someone would have taught it to me.

The model is composed of three basic parts. First, I'll describe how your brain processes emotions (*emotional algebra*), so that we are using the same terms and definitions. Second, I'll tell you the most important thing you should know about emotional algebra (*the secret fact or hidden variable*). I'm going to hold you in suspense. Read on to learn this amazing discovery. . . . Last, I'll walk you through some exercises that can get you started using your combined knowledge of emotional algebra and the fact in a way that completes your understanding of the cognitive model and starts you on your Brain Mechanic journey.

That's it. That's all there is to it. If you're willing to sit and read the next few pages very carefully, and if you take just a few hours to experiment with the exercises, I guarantee you will experience some profound changes in your life.

Emotional Algebra

We are going to start the process by learning what I call emotional algebra. Once you learn how any one emotion works in the cognitive model, you can easily plug different variables into the same general equation.

Let's start with some thought exercises:

We've all seen hidden-camera shows on television. They set up the same gag and run it over and over with different people. Why repeat it? Because every person who walks into the gag reacts differently! They each experience precisely the same setup, or event, but they all have different feelings about that event; and those differing feelings result in many different responses. You can run the same gag all day and keep viewers laughing because you will get different, interesting, and often funny responses.

Imagine the following: Choose any one random seat at a table in a restaurant. Every night at 9:00, walk into the restaurant, approach the predetermined chair, and slap its occupant across the face.

In a year, you will get 365 different reactions. Some people will try to knock your teeth out before you can escape, others will laugh hysterically, others will shrivel in fear, and others will stare intently at their friends for some kind of explanation. The emotions evoked by the slap will vary widely, as will the responses to it. Just like in the hidden-camera shows.

And the slap is only one of countless factors at play here. The demeanor of the slapper, the gender, the dress, the body language, and the environment will all play an important role in what emotion the "slap-ee" experiences following the slap. Did you hear how carefully I worded that? ". . . what emotion the *slap-ee* experiences following the slap." It often appears that events cause emotions, but every slap-ee experienced precisely the same event, yet they felt widely varied emotions following that event. What's going on here? How does this add up?

The first major lesson of emotional algebra is: An emotional feeling, although affected by an event, does not, and cannot, directly result from it. That's right. Write it down on your hand, or your wall, or your notebook, or tattoo it onto your arm. Memorize it:

> An emotional feeling (although affected by an event) does not, and cannot, directly result from it.

The key to every emotional feeling we've ever had or ever will have is not the actual event; rather it lies between the event and the emotion that follows the event:

Event + ? = Emotion

There is something in between the event and the emotion that no one in grammar school ever explained to me. In our hypothetical restaurant scenario, why did some people laugh when slapped by a stranger, why did some feel angry or defensive, and why were others afraid? It was the *exact same stimulus* — why the multitude of responses? The missing piece of this equation is the most important element of emotional algebra we will discuss. The missing piece between events and emotions is beliefs. *Your* beliefs. In psychological circles, beliefs are also called "opinions." Aaron Beck, one of the fathers of CBT, uses the term "core beliefs."

So, our emotional algebra equation is as follows: EV stands for EVENT, and EM stands for our EMOTION; now let B stand for our BELIEFS about the EVENTS (EVs) that happen in our lives:

$$EV + B = EM$$

Returning to the hidden-camera show example, each person received the same slap across the face (EV), but each person had a different belief (B) about the slap, and thus a different emotion (EM) resulted from the exact same slap.

At the heart of the cognitive model lies the wisdom of Epictetus. Epictetus spent his youth as a slave in Rome. Evidently, living at the narrow end of a whip will teach you something about survival psychology.

Epictetus wrote:

Men are disturbed not by things that happen but by their opinions of things that happen.

In other words, the events themselves are not disturbing; rather it is your beliefs about events that create your emotions. Therefore, an emotional feeling, although affected by an event, does not, and cannot, directly result from it. Heard that one before?

In a nutshell, it is nearly impossible to change our emotional responses to some kinds of stress (falling off a cliff, being mugged, finding ourselves in front of a charging bull, treading water as your boat sinks, slamming on the breaks to avoid a collision, "fight-or-flight" stuff) as they are hardwired into the more primitive parts of our brain (more on this later); and we generally can't control the random and potentially disturbing things that happen (EVs) to us every day. Much of life is beyond our control.

Our beliefs determine how we feel about events and situations. Contrary to what you may have always thought, events alone do not cause you to feel any specific emotional response. Your beliefs ultimately determine your emotions. Now that we know our emotional algebra formula is **EV + B = EM**, let's apply it to a few more hypothetical scenarios.

Judy plays the radio at an extremely loud volume while carpooling to avoid talking to her coworker Jake, who she suspects has a crush on her. One morning the radio dies, silencing the car for the drive. Jake is secretly elated, knowing this might be his chance to have an important talk, yet Judy is filled with dread, knowing a conversation she would rather avoid is likely forthcoming.

Both Jake and Judy experience the same event: the radio dying. But it's followed by two very different emotions because their beliefs about the events are different. Only Jake's and Judy's *beliefs* about the radio dying and the implications of those beliefs are capable of determining their emotions: elation and dread, respectively.

Let's try another one. Ken's wife, Carole, took a summer job as a lifeguard. Carole's friend Elayne is throwing a party this Saturday and Carole and Ken are invited. Carole is bummed because she's scheduled to work at the pool that day and will therefore miss the party. Ken is relieved about this, because he finds Elayne's friends too talkative and would much rather go golfing with his buddies than attend the party.

Ken and Carole awake Saturday morning to crashing thunder and a torrential downpour. Elated, Carole knows the pool will close so she can now go to Elayne's. Ken is crushed, because he knows golf is not an option, and he'll be dragged along to the party with Carole.

Did the storm cause Carole to be happy and Ken to be sad? No. That's ridiculous. A rainstorm cannot cause an emotional response. Only a person's *belief* about the storm can determine an emotion. This example illustrates how emotional algebra works. In another example, you may feel anger if you are hosting a pool party and it rains. However, if your house is on fire, a rain shower is a welcome event.

Consider what happens in the ninety seconds after a pilot instructs the crewmembers to prepare the passengers for an emergency landing. Everyone in every single seat hears precisely the same words—but the emotional responses range from calm to visceral screams of panic. Same event, but each passenger has a different belief, thus a different emotion.

Think about this hypothetical case: Someone steals your car. If it was insured (if you *believe* it was insured), and you were sick of that car anyway, then you may feel happy and anticipate a new car at the expense of the insurance company. If, however, you loved that car and/or you know it wasn't insured, you will likely feel depressed or angry.

Remember: EV + B = EM. If the event (EV) is that your mother-in-law will be staying at your house for two weeks, we only need one of the two remaining variables, your belief (B) or your emotion (EM), to determine the third piece of the equation. If you have a high opinion (remember that all opinions are beliefs!) of your mother-in-law and enjoy

spending time with her, then your emotion will be joy, anticipation, and excitement. If, however, you have a low opinion
of her, your emotional response will be dread and irritation.
If you know the first two pieces of the formula, EV and B,
then EM is easily predictable.

And it works the other way as well: if your emotions
(EMs) are revealed by your erupting into sighs of annoyance upon learning that your mother-in-law is coming, I can
discern that your beliefs (Bs) about her are negative.

I've got hundreds of examples, but you get the idea. You
can't cheat emotional algebra. Show me an event, then show
me someone's beliefs about that event and I will tell you what
emotions they will feel. Or show me an event and someone's
emotions about that event, and I can get a good idea of their
beliefs about the same. And remember, opinions are beliefs.

Now that we have a basic understanding of the emotional
algebra equation, and the importance of beliefs (Bs) where
emotions (EMs) are concerned, let's continue with the cognitive model.

Our brains categorize things based on our value system.
Things we like, we call *good*, and things we dislike, we call
bad. We mentally rate everything in our lives: food, movies,
colors, climates, styles, cars, books, ideas, artists, cities,
songs, and so on, and our value or belief system defines
these likes and dislikes.

The Variable in the Equation

Most of your belief system did not originate with you. We
are all products of our culture, families, socioeconomic

backgrounds, religious traditions, geographic locations, and so on. Although you have a personal belief system, you hold thousands of beliefs that you absorbed and inherited from countless sources along the way. There is one thing, however, about your beliefs that you may not know—that no one may have ever told you or shown you.

I'm going to share with you what may be the most important fact you've ever learned. This piece of information was more valuable to me than anything I had previously discovered, and it is the epiphany I found at the center of the cognitive model and CBT.

Are you ready for this? Here's the secret fact revealed:

You can change your beliefs.

There it is: "the fact" that changed the course of my life. You can change your beliefs—any of them—at will, at any time. The only things in the whole universe we have total control over are our beliefs.

"No, that's not possible," you may say.

Oh, but it *is* possible, and over the next few pages, I'm going to prove it and demonstrate to you just how powerful this revelation really is. The following pages will take you from a pre-cognitive life to a post-cognitive life. Welcome to the cognitive revolution—you *can* change your beliefs.

It's a fact. You choose your beliefs. We all do. This in turn means that you have control over them. You don't have to believe you're sitting there reading this book right now if you don't want to. You don't have to believe you even exist, and I've met plenty of people who don't!

You cannot *force* a belief on anyone. It is psychologically impossible to do so. Your beliefs are the most powerful things you have, and they're fluid and changeable. You decide what they are.

No one can force me (or you for that matter) to believe or disbelieve anything. To use an example from Carl Sagan's novel *Contact,* a bunch of thugs could not convince me that my parents don't love me. They could pull out my fingernails, my toenails, and every last tooth in my mouth, and still not change my mind. That is because I believe my parents love me, and more important, I *choose* to believe it. Even if they forced my body into saying it, they could not force my mind into believing it. It's a belief I choose as a matter of fact.

"But I only want to believe what's true," you say. Sorry, but that's not a practical option. You do not, and will not, know the truth all the time, if ever. Your brain fills in a lot of the world contextually—just as your retina fills in the blind spot where your optic nerve connects to the back of your eye: there is a sizable hole in your vision, but your brain fills it in so you don't perceive the hole. Your brain does this exact same thing on a much larger scale with memory and cognition, and it does it on multiple levels. Much of your world is a pastiche of assumptions your brain makes to fill in all the things it doesn't constantly monitor.

We're talking about cognition, not mathematics. Where humans and their emotions and behaviors are concerned, truth is subjective. Is it possible my parents don't love me? Of course it is. Almost anything is possible, but even if something that unlikely were true, you couldn't convince me of it—you could not *make* me believe it.

I believe my parents love me because I've chosen to, and that's the end of it. We will rarely have the luxury of absolute truth, so we choose what we believe—contextually—based on our value system.

The implications of this for our emotional algebra could not be more profound.

Because this equation:

$$EV + B = EM$$

is now this:

$$EV + x = EM$$

There is a *variable* in the equation—over which you have control. Wow. It's true. And it's extremely powerful.

Our beliefs about events are actually variables over which we have tremendous control. Now I understand what Epictetus learned under the whip (event): that he could not control. Epictetus understood the fundamentals of cognitive behavioral therapy—that if he couldn't control being a slave, he could at least control his beliefs about it.

We can believe anything we choose to believe, and once we change our beliefs about an event, our emotional responses thereby change accordingly.

Initially I doubted that I could alter or control my beliefs, but one day, I personally realized this fact was true, and that's when everything began to *change. . . .*

The Politician Voice Effect

A political candidate appeared in an election, announcing his intent to run for office. Let's call this candidate Politician X. I disagreed with his party's platform and I didn't want him to win, and every time he came on television I truly detested the very sound of his voice. I became so angry upon hearing his voice that I would stop whatever I was doing, stand up, find the remote, and mute the television (or throw the remote at the TV). I was brand-new to the cognitive model and the concepts of CBT, and at the mercy of my emotions—adrift on an emotional sea, without an anchor.

I wanted to test some of the concepts I was studying in the piles and piles of psychology books lying around the couch, so I made the conscious decision to use this anger for some experimentation. I told myself, *I cannot change the fact that Politician X is on the air a lot and that I must frequently hear his voice, so I need to find a way to make this situation more tolerable.*

I reminded myself that this candidate's voice was not the real cause of my emotion—it couldn't *cause* my emotion. Rather, my beliefs about his voice were causing me to feel angry. In other words, hello, I was making *myself* angry about this politician!

I knew my emotions (EMs) were being caused by my beliefs (Bs), and I had to change them, but how? What exercise could I use to change my beliefs about his voice?

First, what *were* my beliefs about his voice? Because of his popularity, I believed he was responsible for his party's surge in the polls. I believed that the more he talked with that annoying voice, the higher his party would climb in the polls, and I didn't want them to climb; therefore, I believed that his voice had a causal relationship to my unhappiness.

How in the world could I change that belief, especially when I felt so sure it was true? I assumed that if I was *right* there was no reason to change my belief, because my belief must be right too!

There's no reason for me to change my belief if I'm right! I kept saying to myself. *I'm right! I'm right!*

How utterly *wrong* I was. There *was* a reason to change my beliefs, and it was a very good reason: I wanted to get some emotional relief and let go of the anger I was feeling. So, was there a way to change my belief to a *different* belief that wasn't a *wrong* belief? That's an important distinction.

I knew I couldn't control the course of the campaign, and I wanted to find a way to deal with my anger. I wanted to open my skull with a can opener, take a wrench, and fix my brain, just like a mechanic. And I knew that it was my beliefs I needed to take the wrench to.

But how?

Remember, that's what this book is about — *how*.

My imagination went wild, trying to find a way to change my belief. How was it possible to change a belief that I felt sure was "right"? Is there a different belief that's also right? Or at the very least isn't wrong? Under what hypothetical circumstance would hearing this politician's voice result in a neutral or even positive emotion?

And then, it hit me. I imagined this bizarre scenario:

The phone rings, and I answer and hear: "Hello, I work for XYZ TV as an assistant for the producer of the

Saturday Night Variety Show. We know you've done some
stage work, and you have a good ear. We would like to
pay you $100,000 to consult with us on how best to
impersonate Politician X in some of our skits. We really
think you could help us a great deal. We know you
oppose X's campaign, and your skillful mimicry of the
candidate's mannerisms and vocal idiosyncrasies could
help us lampoon him, thus make him a laughingstock,
and boost his opponent's campaign. So you'd be sup-
porting your own political agenda while making money
and working with some big names in entertainment.
Would you please consider our offer? We will send you
a retainer and about twenty hours of video."

Whoa.

The second I started mentally toying with this admittedly
absurd scenario, my anger melted away. It was like magic. I
forced myself to believe this was a possible scenario and
envisioned it in my mind's eye.

When the politician came on TV, I actually sat there
transfixed by his voice without any negative emotions
(EMs). I replaced my original beliefs (Bs) about his voice
with a new belief (B), based on a fictional, but possible scenario. I listened to him talk and imagined the comedy skits I
helped create surging in popularity on the Internet as the
voting public mocked him and his political platform. Ah,
such sweet victory I'll have if I just sit and study his voice
intently.

Wow. Bang!

The moment I shifted into imagining an "alternate positive scenario," I cured my anger. I kid you not. I *physically* felt the tension in my chest unwind and release through the back of my spine. I *literally* cured my anger.

It was the most profound moment of my life. It was the moment I became my own brain mechanic.

It didn't matter if my imagined story was feasible or would actually happen. Rather, the goal was to contrive a story that would give me some emotional relief from the anger I'd been feeling.

The exercise was a success. The instant that I changed my belief about the voice, I felt a different emotion. By creating an alternative scenario that invoked a positive emotion, I got relief by experiencing a sense of relief and calm from the same stimulus (the politician's voice) that had previously made me angry. Well, of course I did—that's emotional algebra at work. It will work for you too, and you can do it as easily as I did.

In reality, Politician X's voice was no different from Jake and Judy's broken radio or Carole and Ken's rainstorm. It was a neutral stimulus that required me to add my belief to it before it could cause an emotional response. Remember, your beliefs are the variables in the middle of the equation. Only you control the variables—no one else. You have power over them.

By following through on the above exercise and changing my beliefs, I'm practicing cognitive behavior therapy. Here's how *Wikipedia* defines it:

> Cognitive behavioral therapy (or cognitive behavior therapies, CBT) is a psychotherapeutic approach that

aims to influence dysfunctional emotions, behaviors and cognitions through a goal-oriented, systematic procedure.

—*Wikipedia*
http://en.wikipedia.org/wiki/Cognitive_behavioral_therapy

Let me break down this definition for you. The cognitive method "aims to influence dysfunctional emotions . . . through a goal-oriented, *systematic procedure.*" In other words, it aims to change your beliefs in order to change your emotional responses to events. Aha! It makes sense now. Emotional algebra is the *system*, and the *procedure* is the modification of your beliefs. Practicing emotional algebra works wonders for people.

As I stated earlier, my cognitive model using emotional algebra will teach you *how* to change your beliefs about any given event to achieve the desired emotional effect. You can use this method to free yourself from anger, anxiety, panic, rage, depression, worry, jealousy, fear, and so on.

Does that mean CBT guarantees you will never be sad again? No way, that's just not possible. Experiencing perpetual happiness is unrealistic. There are plenty of times sadness and annoyance and regret are necessary, even healthy emotions, but they don't need to evolve into depression, panic, or rage. Contrary to popular belief, CBT is not about "the power of positive thinking." There's room for lots of negative thinking and emotion—just not destructive negative thinking and emotions (another very important distinction, and good news for the curmudgeons and pessimists)!

CBT encourages people to have a full emotional life— good *and* bad emotions. There's a big difference between healthy negative emotions and unhealthy negative emotions. Emotions like frustration, annoyance, regret, irritation, and sadness are healthy negative emotions, but when they turn into anger, rage, depression, hatred, jealousy, or fear, they are unhealthy—destructive—negative emotions.

It is important to have a full emotional life, but with your cognitive skills you can keep normal negative emotions from turning into destructive negative ones. You can be blue instead of black and blue.

Now that you understand the basics of the cognitive model, let's take a moment to look at why it works so well when put to the test in scientific research in Part Two.

Part
Two

THE TUNE-UP:
Change Your Beliefs

I read thousands of pages about all the different parts of the brain, but for the purposes of the Brain Mechanic cognitive model (i.e., emotional algebra), I am going to focus on the function of the following three parts: the prefrontal cortex or PFC, the amygdala, and the cingulate gyrus.

Prefrontal Cortex

Here's how *Wikipedia* defines it:

The prefrontal cortex is the anterior part of the frontal lobes of the brain, lying in front of the motor and premotor areas. This brain region has been implicated in planning complex cognitive behaviors, personality expression, decision making and moderating correct social behavior. The basic activity of this brain region is considered to be orchestration of thoughts and actions in accordance with internal goals. The most typical psychological term for functions carried out by the prefrontal cortex area is executive function. Executive function relates to abilities to differentiate among conflicting thoughts, determine good and bad, better and best, same and different, future consequences of current activities, working toward a defined goal, prediction of outcomes, expectation based on actions, and social "control" . . . Many authors have indicated an integral link between a person's personality and the functions of the prefrontal cortex.

—Wikipedia
http://en.wikipedia.org/wiki/Prefrontal_cortex

Put in laymen's terms, the prefrontal cortex is basically the *executive center* of your brain—the CEO of your company. Your PFC is hugely responsible for your personality. It's mainly the part of your brain we consider *you.* Your PFC is the boss.

Cingulate Gyrus

Take a deep breath before you read this whopper of a definition:

> The cingulate gyrus (a.k.a belt ridge) is a gyrus in the medial part of the brain. It partially wraps around the corpus callosum . . . The cingulate gyrus receives inputs from the anterior nucleus of the thalamus and the neocortex, as well as from somatosensory areas of the cerebral cortex. . . . It functions as an integral part of the limbic system, which is involved with emotion formation and processing, learning, and memory . . . executive control needed to suppress inappropriate unconscious priming is known to involve the anterior cingulate gyrus. It is also involved in respiratory control.
>
> —*Wikipedia*
> http://en.wikipedia.org/wiki/Cingulate_gyrus

To simplify things, think of your cingulate gyrus as the landing on the staircase between the upper and lower parts of your brain. It works like the switch on a train track, or the gearshift in a car. Your cingulate gyrus has the power to change your train of thought. Your cingulate is the part of your brain that allows you to shift from subject to subject, thought to thought, and task to task. When your cingulate gyrus can't shift gears, you feel "stuck"; you're bombarded by "machine-gun thoughts"—those negative thoughts (beliefs!) that you can't seem to stop that cause emotions that feel uncontrollable.

Amygdala

Don't choke on this mouthful:

The amygdalae [plural for amygdala] . . . are almond-shaped groups of nuclei located deep within the medial temporal lobes of the brain in complex vertebrates, including humans. Shown in research to perform a primary role in the processing and memory of emotional reactions, the amygdalae are considered part of the limbic system. . . . The centromedial nuclei are the main outputs for the basolateral complexes, and are involved in emotional arousal in rats and cats. . . . Memories of emotional experiences imprinted in reactions of synapses in the lateral nuclei elicit fear behavior through connections with the central nucleus of the amygdalae. The central nuclei are involved in the genesis of many fear responses, including freezing (immobility), tachycardia (rapid heartbeat), increased respiration, and stress-hormone release. Damage to the amygdalae impairs both the acquisition and expression of Pavlovian fear conditioning, a form of classical conditioning of emotional responses.

—*Wikipedia*
http://en.wikipedia.org/wiki/Amygdala

I call the amygdala the lizard in your head or "lizygdala." This ancient part of the brain processes human animal instincts, like fighting, fleeing, and mating. Actually, the amygdala goes back in time even further than lizards. It's the amphibian in your head. It's *that* deep, *that* old, and *that* important. You can thank your *amphygdala* for the fact you're alive. The primitive emotions and responses generated by your amygdala have saved your life, and your ancestors' lives, more times than you can possibly imagine.

So, anatomically, we have the PFC at the top/front of the brain and the amygdala down in the center of the brain. The cingulate gyrus resides in the middle and serves as the landing on a staircase between the two—with one set of stairs going up to the PFC and another set of stairs going down to the amygdala.

Functional MRI (fMRI) brain imaging shows that emotions, especially primitive feelings like fear and anger, often begin in the amygdala and fire up into the PFC. Irrational amygdala emotions are often at work before our PFC can rationally form beliefs about events. Of course, the stimulus for an emotion can also start in the PFC, because the PFC can imagine all kinds of scenarios that it can send to the amygdala to spark an emotional process; but frequently, emotions begin in the amygdala, and proceed upward/outward.

Functional MRI imaging reveals that our thoughts generally precede our emotions, but sometimes our emotions precede our thoughts. In other words, we can think about something before we feel it, or we can feel the emotion before we think about it.

With an understanding of your brain systems and the cognitive model I've developed, you have the necessary tools to short-circuit dangerous, destructive, or painful emotions. Using the exercises I designed (and ones you create), you possess the tools necessary to experience profound, positive changes in your life.

After practicing exercises for only a few weeks, you'll become your own Brain Mechanic and be an expert at *survival psychology*—getting yourself out of dangerous emotional jams. You will learn how to adapt to your environment by changing your beliefs and, thus, your emotions.

Life is a massive, complex interaction of events, beliefs, and emotions. You have limited control over events and emotions, but you have complete control over your beliefs. That means you have the power to create a constructive, healthy emotional life.

Squashing and Replacing Irrational Beliefs

As I've noted, you can experience both healthy and unhealthy negative emotions. The cognitive model teaches that rational beliefs (RBs) will make you feel healthy negative emotions (disappointed, sorry, annoyed), while irrational beliefs (IBs) create unhealthy negative emotions (anger, depression, panic, and rage). Most important, the cognitive model shows you have the power to change your emotional responses by *squashing* or short-circuiting your irrational beliefs and replacing them with rational beliefs — using emotional algebra.

That's right; we'll squash irrational beliefs (IBs) and replace them with rational beliefs (RBs). A famous psychiatrist named Albert Ellis called the process of changing our beliefs "disputing" or "disputation." In the world of CBT you will hear countless phrases used to describe IBs: *irrational opinions, negative beliefs, negative thoughts, automatic negative thoughts (ANTs), negative opinions, stinkin' thinkin',* and so on.

> We can't always control events and we have limited control over emotions, but we control our beliefs.

Most important: remember that your beliefs cause your emotions. You can't control all the events in your world, therefore you are not responsible for all of them, but you "own" your beliefs and your emotions. They are *all yours*. Write this down and repeat after me: we can't always control events and we have limited control over emotions, but we control our beliefs.

To be sure, changing your beliefs requires work. There is a world of difference between telling yourself something and believing it. But with practice, you can truly and powerfully squash your IBs and replace them with RBs. Through my simple approach to CBT, you will disintegrate the dangerous negative emotions your IBs cause and experience profound emotional relief.

Once you master the skills to squash your IBs and become your own Brain Mechanic, you will forever carry the toolbox to "fix" and face life's challenges. Consider this scenario: Your friends Pat and Kelly are supposed to be coming to stay with you for a whole month. You spend two weeks preparing the house: cleaning, sprucing up, buying food, and arranging the guest quarters. The night of their arrival you light candles in anticipation of their arrival and wait. And wait. As the night wears on you come to realize they're a no-show. Worse, a no-show-no-call.

You are furious because you view their actions as a "terrible" betrayal. You think, *Pat and Kelly are horrible, evil scumbags to screw me over like this!* Take a step back and consider what you are telling yourself. In truth, your belief that their actions are evil and horrible is irrational for a bunch of reasons.

For one thing, you think their bad manners are consciously malicious. Your brain is screaming, *they decided to hurt me!* In reality, their behavior probably has nothing to do with you. Once you take your ego out of the equation, and stop looking at negative events as an intentional, personal attack, it's a lot easier to form rational beliefs about the situation.

In addition, it is important to put the situation into perspective. Pat and Kelly's actions did not put you in harm's way. What they did was not awful. When friends bail on you, it isn't terrible. Genocide is terrible. Being stood up isn't horrible. A plague that kills millions of people is horrible. Cancer is horrible. Thousands of people die in unexpected and gruesome ways every day—and you just got stood up! So what? It's really no big deal. Your house is clean, and the fridge is full. It's highly irrational to assign a strong emotional response—especially an unhealthy negative one—to this event of mere inconvenience.

Albert Ellis calls falling prey to these kinds of irrational beliefs *awfulizing*. People tend to awfulize about all kinds of things that aren't really awful but rather would be more accurately described as annoying or a nuisance. Start listening very carefully to your own and other people's use of the words *terrible, horrible,* and *awful.* You'll find more often than not that the term *annoying* would be better applied. Turn your unhealthy *terrible awfuls* into healthy *annoying nuisances.* Once, when dining out, I heard someone say her salad was terrible. I wanted to ask, "How many people has that salad killed?" Stalin and Mao's regimes were terrible. The most unappealing salad in the world may be wilted, tasteless, or rancid, but not terrible.

As you recognize the language of irrational beliefs in yourself and others, you can learn to avoid making these absurd statements. Consider the following examples:

- He absolutely must be an evil, disgusting sleazebag to treat me so horribly.
- How can she behave so inhumanly and terribly, that vicious witch!
- He's a worthless degenerate to be so awful to everyone and treat me so terribly . . . it's so wickedly unbearable, I can't stand it.
- His asinine behavior was completely unbearable and intolerable.
- What kind of sick, twisted, horrible, insane loser of a person would dare do such a vicious thing?

Write down the irrational belief (IB) language you use most often, and make a conscious decision to avoid it. Pay special attention to what you think and say—pin-pointing when you allow these irrational phrases to infect your daily dialogue with the world. You cannot squash and replace your irrational beliefs (IBs) *until you identify them.* Avoid superlative words such as: *worst, ever, never, forever, always,* and so on. They usually represent exaggerated beliefs.

Get rid of *must.* One of the most common irrational beliefs involves the nonsensical notion of the word *must.* There is no such thing as a *must.*

Ask yourself this very important question: What *must* you do? Really, what *must* you do? Right now, wherever you're sitting—what *must* you do?

Give up?

The answer is . . . *Nothing.* There is nothing you *must* or *have* to do. Bear with me through another hypothetical example to prove my point.

You can go totally limp wherever you're sitting right now. If you live with someone they will find you eventually, motionless on the floor. You don't have to do anything; just lie there.

People will attempt to rouse you. You still don't *have* to do anything. At some point, someone will call an ambulance to take you to a hospital. While there, you continue to remain motionless. Eventually a team of specialists will move you to a facility designed to take care of people who do nothing but lie there. There are plenty of things you *should* do: get up and get on with your life, be a good parent, be honest, work hard, study hard, be kind, participate in life. But all these actions require you to choose to *act* on these behaviors. You don't *have* to live this way; you are not physically *forced* to behave in any given fashion.

While you lie motionless in a home, all your friends will visit for a few weeks and watch you lie there doing nothing. You'll lose your job and probably your house. After a few years, you'll likely lose your spouse, and even your own family will eventually only visit on holidays. You can lie there and do nothing for as long as you choose. Because there are no *musts*.

Then one day after a few years of just lying there, you decide to get up and start talking. You leave the institution and start putting your life back together. At this point you have no money, no clothes, no home, no bank account, no spouse. It may take a few years and some pretty impressive explanations to your friends and family, but you manage to bring them back into your life and gain back their trust. But you can probably forget about your old boss and your old job.

Guess what? You can probably piece your life back together, and you do it faster than you think. Eventually, you'll recover your world, and in a decade no one but the people closest to you will even remember the entire episode. You'll even get a new job, and your world will return to normal.

Even after *all that*, everything will be okay, and who knows, maybe even better than before. This absurd hypothetical example illustrates that believing in *musts* is irrational. Remember: there are no *musts*. You do not have to do anything. *Must* is an illusion. And guess what? Everyone else on this planet enjoys the exact same freedom you enjoy. No one else *must* either!

You heard me right: no one on Earth must *ever* do anything. This includes your waiter, and your maid, and every single one of your employees. This includes your parents, your kids, your coworkers. To believe otherwise is totally irrational. All of your emotional freak-outs about what people must and must not do are irrational and dangerous. Change them. That's your stuff not theirs. Every human is free to act or not to act. We act virtuously by *choice*.

No one must do anything—ever. Remove the concept of *must* from your belief system—*must* in yourself and *must* in others; don't let *must* cause you to suffer emotionally anymore. The sooner you get past the cognitive inflexibility of *must*, the healthier and happier you'll be. Remember that there is no *must*, and *must* has an irrational cousin named "I can't take it."

If you start listening carefully to your own conversations, and the conversations of people around you, you will hear "I can't take it" or "I can't stand it" uttered constantly. It's woven into our dialogue as a normal part of speech, but let's apply logic to the statements and see if they are rational.

You are reading this book right now, therefore you are alive. The fact you are alive is proof that you have never, in your entire life, encountered anything that you could not stand or could not take. Which means all the thousands of times in your life when you said, "I just can't stand x, y, or z," or "I can't take p, d, or q" were wrong. Every time you've ever said these phrases, you turned out to be *wrong*.

You didn't die of your broken heart after that last big breakup, and you didn't die of shame when you threw up on the senior partner. You didn't even die after lying there and doing nothing for a few years while your entire life evaporated around you.

You tolerated it all.

You have taken, withstood, and survived every single challenge and threat you have encountered in life to date. And when the time comes that you encounter something you cannot stand or cannot take, it won't matter anymore, because you'll be dead.

There is nothing you *can't take*.

There is nothing you *can't stand*.

Remove these irrational beliefs from your speech. Albert Ellis rather humorously called these dangerous, irrational beliefs *musterbation* and *icantstandititis*. Listen carefully to yourself for the *I-can't-take* phraseology, and every time you catch it, squash this irrational thought by saying to yourself, "I can stand anything" or "I can take anything." Exaggerate the belief in the other direction for a change. Repeat it to yourself: "I can take anything." You *can* stand it, and you cannot rationally assert otherwise about most things in life. Say it again: "I can stand—anything." The fact you're still alive and reading this book is proof of how tough you really are.

Also, avoid saying or thinking that someone or something *makes* you feel mad, or sad, or any other emotion. Now that you understand emotional algebra, you know that people, things, and events alone are incapable of determining your feelings. They don't *make* you *anything*. How many times a day do we hear "she made me so angry!" or "he made me so sad." Nonsense. Your own beliefs about what she said made you angry, and your beliefs about what he did made you sad. Your beliefs about the people, not the people themselves, created your emotions.

You ultimately determine your feelings based on the

beliefs you embrace and reject. If you fly into an angry rage because you lost a fancy dinner reservation or your dry cleaning was late, this tells you something about your values. It says that missing dinner or not having a pressed shirt is worth getting angry about. It's not. You can believe anything you want about your shirt or your dinner. Choose a belief that results in a healthy emotion.

We know your belief (B) is based on your emotional response (EM) to an event (EV). That's emotional algebra at work. You can't fool it.

Welcome to the cognitive revolution. In a few pages you will be "post-cognitive" and well on your way to profound, positive changes in your life. Feelings stem from your *beliefs* about people, things, and events. Change your internal dialogue and actual speech, so that you remove irrational phrases and locutions. He, she, it, or they cannot *make* you feel anything; what you *believe* can make you experience an emotion.

Be forewarned: You will never have total control over your emotions. *Never.* Plenty of them will begin in your amygdala—before your PFC gets a crack at sorting through them—but once you feel and identify your emotions (EMs), you then have a *choice:* to analyze your emotions (EMs) rationally and work on changing your beliefs (Bs) or to surrender to the irrational lizygdala signals and be washed away on an emotional sea, out of control.

The cognitive model demonstrates that you have a choice. You have a choice: to fight or to surrender to lizygdala. You have a choice: to think or to blank out.

A few weeks ago when I awoke one morning, I became

conscious (before even opening my eyes) that I was already in a wretched mood. Wow, how can I feel *this* crappy *this* early? I don't even have my eyes open yet! That word "feel" got me *thinking . . . I know that my feelings are tied to my beliefs, so I wonder what I might already believe about this morning that has me in this mood. What do I believe about today's schedule or last night's sleep. . . ?*

I started working through my emotional algebra before I even opened my eyes:

$$EVs + Bs = EMs$$

I kept thinking, and thinking, and thinking, until: bang! My emotions started changing.

The very process of walking yourself through the steps of emotional algebra will give you a sort of foot in the door to rational thoughts. Once you get that foot in there, and get a peek of your thinking process (or *cognition*!), you will start to teach yourself how to find the cognitive results you want.

"Sounds like you're talking about some kind of mind control," you say.

And how.

Mozart, Isaac Newton, Albert Einstein, Michael Jordan, Lance Armstrong, Warren Buffet, Bill Gates, Oprah Winfrey, Abraham Lincoln, Mother Teresa, Nelson Mandela, Galileo — all *masters* of mind control.

You bet I'm talking about mind control. That's the whole ball game. That's what separates human beings from wild animals. However, let me be clear: I'm talking about *self* mind control.

- Controlling your own mind is virtue.
- Controlling someone else's mind is vice.
- Controlling your beliefs is the ultimate control.

When you start working with beliefs, you're doing the heaviest cognitive lifting possible. You are working at the deepest level in your brain. You are rebuilding your *foundation* when you rebuild your beliefs. Your beliefs (Bs) form your personality, so changing them changes your relationship to the world and the people in it.

You want a better personality? Get better beliefs. You want to behave better? Choose better beliefs. You want better friends and a better job? Get yourself a better belief system. You want a better marriage? Change your beliefs. Want a better body? Change your beliefs about working out. You want satisfaction out of life? Change your beliefs about what will make you happy. The process is that simple. I kid you not.

Finally, it's very important that you understand why I titled this book *The Brain Mechanic*. Nobel laureate Dr. Eric Kandel is one of many neuroscientists to prove that cognitive processes can literally—*physically*—alter the shape of structures in the brain. Many people think that psychotherapy is based on some intangible, ethereal world of thoughts and ideas—with no physical effect on the brain. But that's not the case.

You can *physically alter* the structures in your brain—without cutting open your skull and using surgical instruments to manipulate the cells. That's what Dr. Kandel and many of his colleagues have proven. So when I say *Brain Mechanic*, I mean you can literally use these tools to *physically* fix parts of your brain—just like an auto mechanic *physically* works on engine parts under the hood. The auto mechanic usually has to open the hood to work on a car engine, but through cognitive therapy, you can work on your brain without opening your skull. This stuff is *that* powerful!

Okay, you've done the hard part and learned the cognitive model. Now comes the fun part. Let's move on to the exercises so you can start playing with your powerful new cognitive toys—and changing your brain to build a better, stronger you.

> "Out of our beliefs are born deeds; out of our deeds we form habits; out of our habits grows our character; and on our character we build our destiny. . . ."
> —HENRY HANCOCK

Part
Three

BRAIN MECHANIC TOOLBOX:
Exercises for Living

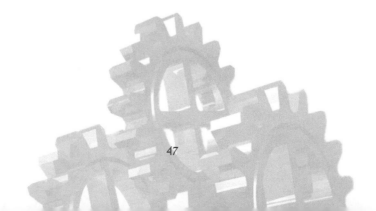

We all know how to get to Carnegie Hall . . . practice. Success in most endeavors includes a great deal of practice. When it comes to fixing your brain, practice is key. The more you practice, the better and more effective you'll become. It doesn't make any sense to wait around and do nothing until the day of the recital. Don't wait until you're hit with a whopper of an emotional disturbance to start practicing your cognitive skills. Hit the gym now, every day, all day, and you'll be ready when the tough events happen. Here are some exercises that will start strengthening your brain. The harder you work at these, the easier they get, and the stronger you'll be.

Fat Tummy Breath

I cannot overemphasize the importance of breathing correctly and the positive effect it can have on brain function. Truth be told, most of us don't breathe right. We live in a thin-obsessed world. Although average people are heavier than ever, our celebrity role models are all tiny, and every month a new diet or exercise machine hits the infomercial circuit. One result of this constant pressure to be slim is what I call *The Great Sucking-In.*

I do it all the time, and so do you. We want to look young, fit, and trim, so we suck in our stomachs. Some people spend hours camouflaging their tummies and tugging on their shirts, in an unsuccessful attempt to hide their fat.

The Great Sucking-In makes our chests puff out and inflate, and keeps us breathing up high in our bodies, while the *fat tummy breath* allows us to breathe deeper in our being. Fat tummy breathing is a critical part of the entire cognitive process. Don't just read through my description and do it in your imagination (like I do when I read books like this), actually do it —*physically*. If you think it looks embarrassing, you can practice in private, but don't cheat.

Here goes:

Forget about your chest — totally forget it. Concentrate on the fattest part of your tummy — down low where your diaphragm and belly button are. Hold your hand on your belly and push that part of your tummy out slowly, as you draw air deep into your body. Ignore your chest and push out your tummy.

Hold your hand over your abdomen and imagine you are pulling your belly out. Feel the air going deep into your lungs, into your diaphragm, and then exhale slowly.

Now, do it again, inhaling even more deeply this time. Make your tummy get fatter. Forget your chest and shoulders, and push your diaphragm out with a deep, fat tummy breath. Remember, this is not a military drill. Done correctly, this breathing exercise should make you look fat, round-shouldered, and dumpy. Your goal here is the opposite of sexiness. Do it really well, and it may even make you look pregnant.

Now that you've gotten the hang of it, take your time and inhale for six seconds, making your tummy as fat as you can make it, and then exhale for three to five seconds. Repeat this breathing exercise, inhaling for six and exhaling for three to five seconds. Practice this until you're an expert and are able to take three deep, fat tummy breaths in any location, under any circumstances. Become a master of the fat tummy breath; it's a critical part of survival psychology.

Crystal Ball

Based on the simple fact that no one knows the future, the crystal ball exercise works wonders on anger and is great for eliminating anxiety too.

Remember Judy and Jake who were commuting in the car together? If you are Judy, you dread a conversation with Jake because you think he has a crush on you that isn't mutual. You worry that silence in the car will lead Jake to declare his feelings for you, and, in turn, you will have to reject him. Then he will avoid you at work, maybe even resent you or, worse yet, bad-mouth you. At the very least, the situation at work would become awkward. You don't like rejecting people, and you're panicking about the fact that the radio died, because now you're trapped in the car for thirty minutes in a position you find uncomfortable.

In fact, all your irrational beliefs (IBs) about this bad situation are really just conjecture. You do know that the radio died, but you don't know *for sure* that Jake has a crush on you. Even if he does, you don't know that he's going to pick today to confess his attraction, and if he does, you don't know that this would necessarily be a bad thing. There are a thousand potential outcomes to this situation, many of which are positive.

Maybe Jake *does* have a crush on you, and you *will* have to reject him, but he could take it really well, and you both could become great friends once the air has cleared. Maybe he won't take it well, but the extra five minutes you spend fiddling with the broken radio could save you from getting into a bad car accident a mile up the road.

The point is, you're not omniscient, so you don't know what will happen next. If you're Judy in this situation, force yourself to imagine some positive outcomes that could result from the broken car radio. For starters, you can finally justify installing the CD player you've always wanted since the old unit is broken. That's an upside, isn't it? Remember, when you imagine a positive outcome instead of a negative one, you can begin to short-circuit your negative emotions before they take over.

We all experience road rage at one time or another. The crystal ball exercise works extremely well at handling this predicament. Consider the basic traffic jam. You're driving down a narrow one-way street and you come to a service truck that is sitting with its hazard lights on, blocking the entire street. Arrrrgh! Immediately, irrational thoughts start firing up from your lizygdala, through your cingulate, and into your PFC: *What kind of idiotic, obnoxious moron would dare park in the middle of the street? Does this arrogant @$#! have an engraved invitation from the mayor to park here?! I can't stand it! This fool cannot actually be doing this. He* must *move, and he* must *move* now!

You recognize the anger and *must* language of irrational beliefs from a mile away, but now, instead of sitting in your car fuming, you have a better way to deal with the situation.

Now you have the Brain Mechanic cognitive model: First, take your fat tummy breath. Always take a fat tummy breath

immediately when you sense an emotional disturbance com-
ing(!). Then work your crystal ball exercise—tell yourself: *I
do not know the future,* and consider the following possibility or
one of your own choosing:

Without the three-minute delay in your travels caused by
the offending truck, you could have been seven blocks farther along in your trip when another car could have backed
out of an alley and smashed into you precisely at the moment
you passed by—crash! You could have been injured or
dead.

You see, it is actually possible that this seemingly frustrating delay could have saved your life. Perhaps considering
this alternative scenario seems silly, but think about how
many times you've looked at things from the opposite (read:
negative) perspective. After losing your keys you may have
thought: *If only I had checked to make sure the keys were in my
purse before leaving the house, I'd have saved a hundred dollars in
locksmith fees. If only I had reached into my purse for a breath mint
like I usually do (when I carpool), I would have noticed the missing
keys. If only today had been a carpool day, I would have looked for
that breath mint and saved a hundred bucks!*

You see how these "sliding doors" alter the directions our
lives take.

We know the old saw "hindsight is 20/20," but the future
is a radically different variable in which we can envision
many different outcomes. Bizarre, desultory, and totally
random paths propel us through life—leading us through
feast and famine, safety and danger.

Consider the following true scenario: On the morning of
September 11, 2001, *Family Guy* creator Seth MacFarlane

was scheduled to fly to Los Angeles from Boston on American Airlines Flight 11. Suffering from a hangover and having been told the wrong departure time (8:15 AM instead of 7:45 AM), MacFarlane arrived at the airport around 7:30 AM and was told he couldn't board the flight because the gates were closed. Fifteen minutes after takeoff, the plane was hijacked and flown into the World Trade Center, leaving no survivors.

MacFarlane was incredibly lucky, but who would have believed fate was on his side when he missed his flight that day? On any given day, small, seemingly insignificant choices and actions can lead to fortune or disaster. And, because we do not know the future, it is highly irrational to assign a firm, fixed belief (emotion) to any specific event.

We have no way of knowing whether today's disaster will be tomorrow's salvation, or if today's misery is tomorrow's joy. If you had a crystal ball, you would see that all too often we have narrowly escaped death or tragedy and never even realized it.

The next time you find yourself caught in a traffic jam, fully engage your PFC in the crystal ball exercise and squash the irrational emotional signals coming up from your lizygdala.

Say it aloud if you need to: "For all I know, this schmuck blocking the road might be saving a life. Maybe if I wasn't delayed here I would have been in an accident myself a few minutes from now. It is totally irrational for me to have such a strong emotional response to a traffic delay. I can and will *choose* to believe that this delay is actually going to lead me into good fortune. Maybe the love of my life will crash their bike into me because I'm delayed here. . . ."

Highly unlikely, yes, but it is possible. Belief in the mere possibility is all you need to start feeling the changes.

Next, replace your old irrational belief (IB) with a rational belief (RB), and you will feel your emotions (EMs) change. That is the power of CBT. And who knows, your alternate rational scenario might actually happen someday. It truly *is* a possibility, thus it is irrational to preclude it.

As soon as you change your assumptions about things that upset you, you will change your emotional response. I use this exercise daily as a driver, constantly forcing myself to believe that whatever happens in traffic will lead to the best possible conclusion. It's changed my driving life and probably added years in stress relief. I don't sweat delays anymore because I change my beliefs about them. It's that simple.

An exercise like the crystal ball could also help with the Pat and Kelly houseguest scenario. Maybe Pat and Kelly have become huge party animals since you've last seen them. Maybe they would have kept you up all night and invited shady guests who would have stolen your departed grand-mother's jewelry and trashed your new walnut floors. It's entirely possible that you just dodged a huge bullet.

Or maybe because Pat and Kelly bailed on you, you will accept an invitation to a dinner party and meet the love of your life and get married and have kids. For all we know, you might be sitting somewhere seven years from now, saying, "Wow, just imagine what would have happened if Pat and Kelly would have shown up that weekend! I never would've met my spouse and had my children. Thank goodness they blew me off! I can't imagine how lonely and empty my life would now be if they had actually shown up. Here's a toast to Pat and Kelly for standing me up that weekend!"

That's the crystal ball exercise in a nutshell. Since you do not know the future, you cannot rationally assign a negative emotion to a circumstance because that event might actually result in a positive outcome.

In fact, you not only do not know the future, you also most often lack pertinent information about the present. For example, you may think you hear a stranger bad-mouth you on the street when the person is actually talking to someone else on a Bluetooth. When a cute girl declines a date with you, you may assume it's because you're bald when she is secretly involved with her married coworker.

And remember how frustrated you were when the delivery truck was blocking the street? What if the driver had stopped there to rescue an old lady who collapsed to the ground right in that truck's path?

"That's absurd," you say.

Not really. You are exercising your brain just like you exercise your body by doing push-ups. You don't do push-ups to get anywhere, you do them to strengthen your arms. Strengthen your brain by changing your beliefs.

> Anger stems from irrational beliefs about others, and anxiety stems from irrational beliefs about yourself.

Some people may consider this crystal ball approach an exercise in "positive thinking," but the process of "positive thinking" only scratches the surface. Using the Brain Mechanic cognitive model serves as a weapons-grade version of "the power of positive thinking"—it's the power of training your brain to *believe.*

We have seen how the crystal ball exercise works to eliminate negative emotions including anger; now I have something fantastic (and even more intriguing) to share with you. Write this down and memorize it: anger stems from irrational beliefs about others, and anxiety stems from irrational beliefs about yourself.

What this means is feelings of anger result from irrational beliefs about other people (the language of *must* is a tip-off); and feelings of anxiety result from irrational beliefs about yourself. In addition, feelings of panic stem from beliefs about yourself, and feelings of rage stem from your thoughts about others. The belief that the person behind you must not bump the back of your chair again makes you angry. The belief that you must lose weight before your high school reunion makes you anxious. The belief that the new neighbors must invite you to their barbeque, and don't, makes you angry. The belief that you must make it through a traffic jam in record time makes you anxious. The belief that someone cutting you off in traffic is awful makes you angry. You get the idea.

Make a list of beliefs that have caused you to feel anger, anxiety, panic, and rage in the past. Now, list some rational beliefs with which you can replace those irrational beliefs.

Whenever you feel a pang of anxiety coming, look for the must about yourself—"I must attend every party I'm invited to" . . . "I must impress total strangers in a disco with my wardrobe" . . . and so on.

Whenever you feel a pang of anger, look for the must about others. "The clerk must say 'you're welcome' after I say 'thank you' . . . "My date must notice my new hairdo, or he isn't really into me."

He must/she must/they must is an IB that will make you angry. I must/I mustn't is an IB that will make you anxious.

Alternative Positive Scenario

As I learned with the politician voice effect, one of the easiest ways to change our beliefs (and thus, our emotions) about an event is to create a hypothetical scenario in which the exact same event leads to different feelings.

Once we consciously recognize that our emotions about an event are fluid and not predetermined or unchangeable, we can easily gain perspective and replace our irrational, negative beliefs with rational, positive ones.

I succeeded in eliminating my irritation with Politician X and his voice by imagining a situation in which I would want to hear and study his voice to make him lose the election rather than associating it with him winning the election.

Feel free to get creative with this exercise, as I did. When you perceive an unwelcome event, consciously try to come up with an imaginary scenario in which the exact same event would be acceptable, even enjoyable, and would result in a positive outcome (or, at the very least, not a negative one).

Maybe you find yourself frustrated while searching aimlessly for a parking space at a crowded mall. Using the Alternative Positive Scenerio exercise, imagine yourself on a reality game show in which you have the painless task of locating a parking spot to win big money, while your game show opponent must handle a deadly snake to win the prize.

Lucky you! Not only do you *not* have to deal with poisonous snakes today, you even get a fat paycheck at the end if you win the competition. Okay, yes, it's just a fantasy, but the exercise allows you to consider a new belief just long enough for the rational part of your brain to recognize a potential positive outcome. No matter the situation, given the right incentive, you could endure anything.

You could also consider the positive outcome that you escaped some unpleasant fate by not finding a nearby spot. Maybe parking where you did prevented you from encountering a bargain-hunting stampede by the front door. You could also think of the benefits of parking far away. You get some great exercise while walking from the outer world parking lot. Usually you pay your health club a bunch of money every month for this privilege, but today you'll experience a nice fresh-air workout, and you don't even have to worry about foot fungus or lines for the treadmill. Not only that, you'll burn so many calories while carrying your heavy shopping bags back to the car, that now you can eat a cookie without feeling guilty. If the walk is long enough, and the mall is sufficiently crowded, you might even meet someone cute along the way.

The Alternative Positive Scenario offers a benefit beyond changing your beliefs. Just the act of thinking through possible alternatives will often *buy you enough time* to escape the negative emotion and walk through emotional algebra. You heard that right. Thinking (which is the essence of cognitive exercise) buys you time to figure out how to best escape emotionally dangerous situations. Start thinking through your cognitive exercise long enough to remove yourself from a potentially explosive situation. Leave the event (EV), regroup, and come back to it. By then, you'll defuse your reaction *before* unhealthy negative emotions (EMs) ignite.

The Alternate Positive Scenario exercise is great for cutting off feelings of annoyance before they turn into anger or rage, and with a little creativity and practice, you can imagine a potential rational upside to almost any situation. Herein lies the power of the cognitive model, and you are now becoming your own Brain Mechanic.

Exploding Point

There's a television show in which people are subjected to annoying situations to see how long it takes them to explode in anger, or boil over. Next time you are stuck in a really long line at a store, or dealing with an incredibly slow and/or incompetent clerk, first take a fat tummy breath. Then remind yourself that you cannot know for sure that you aren't on a hidden camera show. Sure, the odds are remote, but they exist. What percentage of the people on those shows knew they were on one of them? Maybe you've walked into a new reality show in which Bill Gates is giving away houses to people who have the patience of saints, and your *not* losing your cool will soon be rewarded with new digs. There are a hundred scenarios you can dream up to find a reason to keep your cool. So do it. It doesn't matter if they're true, only *possible*.

This, again, is the power of the cognitive model—you have a choice. Once you start working through cognitive scenarios, you will feel your emotions changing as you think. Rational beliefs will cause healthy emotions—both positive and negative. Irrational beliefs will cause unhealthy emotions. People, places, and events cannot cause your emotions—your beliefs can. Epictetus taught us that centuries ago.

Am I suggesting that you should deliberately delude yourself into thinking you're on television? No, of course not. That's absurd. I'm saying that if you will simply go through the cognitive process of *considering* it as a rational possibility (which it *is!*), you will buy yourself a few extra seconds of rational cognition before any strong emotions from your lizygdala hijack your cingulate loop and start overheating your brain. In those few extra seconds, you can use emotional algebra to replace your irrational beliefs (IBs) with powerful, rational ones, escape the emotional disturbance, and prevent the thought from getting stuck in your cingulate, stuck, stuck, stuck, stuck, stuck. Taking a fat tummy breath and replacing your irrational belief with an alterative positive one will stop the stucks.

Once you've acknowledged that it's simply *possible* that you are on a hidden camera show, literally look around for the cameras. I know it sounds silly, but try it anyway.

I can already hear the detractors: "He's just saying live in a state of denial about everything—an imaginary state of 'positive-thinkity-think' denial."

No. I'm saying use your imagination and your cognitive flexibility to create a healthy emotional life instead of an unhealthy one. The imagination is a wonderful and powerful place, and you can use it to your great benefit—especially in your emotional world.

Your imagination has evolved to protect you. Tons of brain research shows that the physical structure of the brain called the ventromedial prefrontal cortex (or VMPC) is responsible for what is known as a "religious" experience or "faith." You don't need to believe in God to make use of the VMPC to improve your life. The cognitive model shows the "nonspiritual" how to engage the "spiritual" part of their brains. Richard Dawkins, the most vocal champion of atheism, could use this model just as effectively as the Pope. The cognitive model works as well for the devoutly religious as for the devoutly nonreligious.

The goal of the exploding point exercise is to start considering alternate, rational possibilities, and to force yourself to believe that they *are* possibilities. By doing this, you avoid the negative emotions that come from believing irrational things.

Superstar *Shush*

People often attempt to excuse their emotional outbursts by claiming, "I just couldn't take it anymore," "I reached my breaking point," or "He pushed me too far!" Are these legitimate, rational statements?

Let's see how lame these excuses are. Think back to the last time you lost control of your emotions. Where were you? And what happened? Now think of the people whom you most admire and respect in the world or in front of whom you would be totally humiliated if you made a scene—say, for instance, your favorite movie or rock star. Who would blow up at a store clerk if you were standing in line with Angelina Jolie or your favorite president? Not likely.

Before I became my own Brain Mechanic, I had my buttons pushed while waiting in line at an electronics store. The store clerk claimed I couldn't get a refund for my computer, because there was a different policy regarding laptops. We argued for ten minutes—I told him the sales clerk had clearly explained the policy, and he said that particular clerk clearly didn't understand the policy anyway. We went back and forth and I raised my voice, demanding to talk to the regional manager. It was an ugly scene. My personal idol is television host Charlie Rose. Now, with my newfound Brain Mechanic tools, I would imagine how I would respond in the situation if Charlie Rose would've walked in the door right before I barked at the service clerk. The *last* thing in the world I would have done was lose my cool with the clerk in front of Charlie Rose! I would never let him see me act like a child.

This exercise demonstates we *can* control our emotions when we *choose* to control our beliefs. Under virtually any circumstance, anyone can keep their cool. There is no such thing as "I just couldn't control myself." That is an age-old irrational belief, and it's nonsense.

You *can* control yourself, as long as you *choose* to control yourself. Before you bark at the clerk, take a fat tummy breath and imagine your favorite celebrity walking through the door. Anyone (including you!) can keep your act together if the motivation is right.

This is all about your will. Your will is in your PFC. Your beliefs are in your PFC. You have control over your beliefs and the executive center of your brain; you are, in fact, the executive—the Big Boss. Your PFC is the CEO of your brain, and your cingulate is your executive assistant—running errands through your brain. Next time you feel the overpowering urge to snap at someone, take your fat tummy breath, and then use the exploding point exercise: imagine that your personal role model is standing right beside you, watching you and telling you to be cool and "shush."

You will discover that you *do* have the power to keep it together.

No Boomerangs

Anxiety breeds anxiety. Anger breeds anger.

The second we feel certain emotions, we feel bad about the fact that we feel them, which only serves to intensify them. That's what happens in a panic attack. People feel a little anxious, and get anxious about that feeling, and then that added anxiety makes them even more anxious, which turns into panic. I call the effects of these intensified feelings *boomerang emotions*. The way to avoid them is to initially force yourself to accept any emotion your lizygdala fires at your PFC.

Feelings such as anger and anxiety coming from the lizygdala can get stuck in the cingulate and start reinforcing themselves in a vicious cycle. But you can break this cycle before it gets out of control by acknowledging what is going on when you first feel a disturbing emotion. You don't want these dangerous emotions to boomerang back and forth—

like a never-ending ping-pong game between your lizygdala and your PFC—with your cingulate gyrus stuck in the middle and overheating.

When uncomfortable feelings start creeping in, tell yourself:

- It's okay to feel anxious. That's my lizygdala at work.
- It's okay to feel fear; my amygdalae are protecting me.
- That pang of jealousy is okay; it's my lizygdala.
- I accept that surge of anger; it's only my amygdala.
- I'm grateful my lizygdala is working properly.

Your immediate acceptance of dangerous emotional impulses will keep you from panicking and getting the emotion stuck in a self-reinforcing irrational cingulate cycle. Accept the initial bursts of amygdala emotions. Once you have accepted the amygdala signal, you can then engage in a rational argument with your PFC. This simple action allows you to counteract the irrational emotions firing up from lizygdala with rational, calming beliefs sent down from your PFC. An important exercise, No Boomerangs is the second step in the Five-Step Quick Survival guide (see page 95) I designed to rebuild my own brain.

Machine-Gun Rational Thoughts

After warding off boomerang emotions, it's time to fire back from your PFC to short-circuit that cingulate cycle and eliminate any emotional disturbance. Remember: When your amygdala fires a dangerous signal up to your PFC, if that signal encounters an irrational belief (IB) in your PFC, that irrational belief will reinforce and strengthen the dangerous signal and send it right back into the loop (more powerful than it was the first time). But, if the amygdala signal encounters a rational belief (RB) in your PFC, that rational belief will weaken and disrupt the signal. The more filled with rational beliefs your PFC is, the faster you will short-circuit a dangerous cingulate cycle. You can use this machine-gun rational thoughts exercise to avoid overheating. Here's how to do it.

Man your mental machine gun and fire away at your irrational beliefs (IBs) with some of the rational beliefs (RBs) below or come up with your own. Don't stop with the artillery. Just keep shooting and shooting. Blast those harmful irrational beliefs (IBs) out of your PFC. Say them aloud if you need to or write them down:

- It's silly for me to believe that. Everything will end for the best. There is no must.
- I'll turn these lemons into lemonade. I have always survived. There is no must. I will get through. There is no must. I have withstood everything that's come my way.
- As long as I keep breathing everything will be fine. Those thoughts are irrational and unrealistic. I know emotional algebra, and I control my beliefs. I don't believe those irrational thoughts because I don't have to.
- I know things will eventually work out for the best, regardless of what happens now.
- There are no musts. I can take anything. Every moment of adversity is an hour in my cognitive gym.

Stretch. Evolve. Bend.
Move. Absorb. Adapt.
Inhale. There are no
musts.

- The future holds fantastic things. I will survive, overcome, and thrive. I refuse to believe irrational thoughts. Challenges are opportunities to change my beliefs.

> "The destiny of every human being is decided by what goes on inside his skull when confronted with what goes on outside his skull."

- Darwin was right—adaptation is the key to survival.
- It's silly to let these circumstances inform my emotions. I am a rational being. I control my beliefs.

You get the idea. If these are too schmaltzy and you can't relate to them, make up your own, and make them way cool. Create and use machine-gun rational thoughts to strengthen your beliefs, thus your PFC—thus, *you*.

The famous psychiatrist Dr. Eric Berne wrote, "The destiny of every human being is decided by what goes on inside his skull when confronted with what goes on outside his skull."

You exist in two distinct worlds conveniently delineated by a solid barrier called your "skull." The physical world exists outside your skull, bound concretely by mathematics, physics, and all hard sciences. The metaphysical world exists inside your skull and is ruled by psychology, faith, religion, superstition, and ideology. And, yes, the world inside is also *partly* governed by physical laws, but the general distinction holds true.

Your *belief system* is the *interface* between those two worlds—the goings-on inside (cognition/emotion) and outside (events) your skull. This interface determines how smoothly both worlds coexist. The more absolute and irrational your belief system, the more painful and disturbing the interface between the worlds will be. The more flexible and rational your belief system, the smoother the interface will be—resulting in emotional calm and well-being.

People frequently combat emotional disturbances with recreational or prescription drugs. These substances work from the bottom area of the brain up to the PFC. Cognitive behavioral therapy, on the other hand, works from the PFC *down*. And we all know it's easier to slide downhill than climb uphill. That's a metaphor, of course, but it truly is easier to fix your brain from your PFC down than to work from your brain stem up. You can keep pumping drugs up through your blood-brain barrier or start sending rational beliefs down to your lizygdala from your executive center. You are your PFC, the CEO of your brain.

Combining the No Boomerangs exercise and the Machine-Gun Rational Thoughts exercise is one of the most powerful cognitive skills I have learned. Anytime your amygdala throws an irrational belief (IB) at you, hit it with a Machine-Gun Rational script. Whenever you feel a burst of negative emotion coming up from your lizygdala, *FIRE!*

Brain Talk

Now that you understand the cognitive model and some functional brain anatomy, you can speak from the appropriate part of your brain at the appropriate time. You know emotions begin deep in the lizygdala and then move up toward your PFC. Using this knowledge, you can "talk" from those two specific parts of your brain.

Here's a personal example: Last year I developed a crush on a near-stranger who was married. Initially, every meeting felt awkward, but then I learned the cognitive model and some brain anatomy, and that taught me how to talk from different places in my brain.

Let's listen to the conversations going on in the different parts of my brain in response to my mad crush:

I fell in love with you seven minutes after I met you and I will love you forever. Your husband nauseates me. I hate being in the same room with you if I can't kiss you and smell your neck. I am so in love with you I can hardly stand it. Every time the phone rings, I hope that it's you. Every song lights me up with waves of emotion about you. I am amygdala, and I feel like eating, fighting, and living for you

—Lizard Brain (my amygdala)

I hardly know you, and I may never know you. You have a life and a husband, and you may not even care that I exist. No matter how much lizygdala fires these emotional feelings, it will not guide my life; it will not direct my actions. The emotions coming from my amyg-dala are irrational and dangerous vestiges of amphibian evolution. I have control over my beliefs, and I refuse to believe the signals from my amygdala. I am not in love

with you. I choose my beliefs and my actions based on
rational thought. My feelings of love for you are irrational and they will not run my life. I am my prefrontal
cortex, and I am the boss.

—Boss (prefrontal cortex or PFC)

Both of the above statements are totally true, but they are
true in different parts of your brain. I can choose to listen to
either part of my brain. The choice is mine, and it can be
yours, too. When people act on messages they hear coming
from their amygdala they can destroy marriages, families,
friendships, careers, businesses, dinner parties, and tropical
vacations. The key is to focus on and act upon what your
PFC tells you!

Once you buy this book for everyone you love (ahem!),
you will speak the common language of the cognitive model,
and you will be able to communicate with each other more
effectively by talking from the appropriate parts of your
brains. I cannot overstate how critical communication is and
how important sharing the Brain Mechanic language and
tools are to this end.

Teach the basic Brain Mechanic anatomy to everyone
close to you. Then you can say, "Okay, I want to talk to you
from two different parts of my brain. First, I will tell you
what my amygdala *feels*, then I'll tell you what my PFC
believes, and then I will need your help in reinforcing my
rational beliefs and squashing my irrational emotions.
Because I'm feeling angry, but I know I have no reason to
be. . . ." See how vital this is? Brain Mechanic communication changes *everything*.

People sound jumbled and crazy when they try to talk from their PFC and amygdala simultaneously. When you're feeling angry about a situation with a loved one, talk from the rational part of your brain. Don't let your lizygdala lash out and hurt the people close to you. When you're writing dialogue for the bad guy in your new novel, unleash all the emotional venom you want—in the safe confines of fiction. Keep lizydala in check when you're in front of the judge, but when your shrink says "tell me exactly how you feel"—then you can unlimber all the messy emotional artillery and fire away! Talk from the appropriate part of your brain at the appropriate time. And when you're at the office, don't let your amygdala have any conversations with your boss.

Like Everyone

I've never met anyone I didn't like. Seriously. I know it sounds radical, but it's true. I like everyone, because I don't confuse people with their belief systems. You will find that you can like everyone too—if you separate people from their beliefs.

Every baseball fan knows if you are a southside Chicagoan, you love the White Sox and revile the Cubs. Northsiders religiously root for the Cubs and despise the White Sox. Rivalry between the two teams has existed for years, and even fans break out in bloodly brawls in the name of the game. If a die-hard White Sox fan grew up a few miles north and was raised to love the Cubs, would the Cubs suddenly become a better team or more worthy of support? Of course not; that's silly. Only the fan's *beliefs* about who was the best team would be different.

In reality, the moment of conception and the vagaries of the fallopian lottery shape your beliefs; they are accidents of birth, geography, and socioeconomic status. Parents, politicians, and religious leaders help you form a belief system. Remember that most of your belief system is not original to you—it's been given to you by your culture, family, education, society, and so on.

People generally hold religious beliefs for the same reason they become Sox fans or Cubs fans. A child born to devout Muslim parents in Saudi Arabia grows up with strong beliefs in Islam. A child born to fundamentalist Christian parents in Texas grows up with strong beliefs in Christianity. A child born to Hindu parents in Mumbai grows up with strong beliefs in Hinduism. A child born to Buddhists in Bangkok holds Buddist beliefs. If you switched any of these children at birth, they would grow up to hold the same beliefs as their new parents—and hold them just as zealously. As with anything, there are exceptions—northside Sox fans, for example. You could call these people converts, which simply means they *changed their beliefs*. People change their beliefs for an infinite number of reasons. CBT shows you how to change them for emotional relief from dangerous negative emotions.

Use your working knowledge of the cognitive model to separate people from their beliefs. In most cases, a Sox fan and a Cubs fan were simply born in different neighborhoods. It's ridiculous to like or dislike someone because of team loyalties, especially when anyone at any time is free to change sides! (I know some hard-core sports fans would beg to differ, but you get the idea). Most people are as deeply convinced of the truth or correctness of their beliefs as you are of the truth of yours. But people are *not* their beliefs. They often hold them for random, meaningless reasons, and they can change them at any time.

Beliefs are not tattoos, they are just like clothes—you can put them on and take them off at will. For instance, if you're on the political left, you may have been a big fan of Dennis Miller, who has made a clear shift to the right. Now you may think, *I don't like him anymore. What is wrong with him, has he lost his mind?!* No, he hasn't lost his mind. He simply changed his belief system. It's not personal. Dennis Miller is still a smart, funny guy; you're just annoyed by his current, right-leaning belief system. If someday he changes his beliefs to match yours, you'll probably like him again.

Remember, the brain instinctually categorizes your likes as "good" and dislikes as "bad." But your like or dislike of something only means that thing is good or bad according *to you*. It doesn't mean it's objectively good or bad.

Learn not to judge people as good or bad based on their likes and dislikes. You're not the arbiter for everyone else. One man's trash is another's treasure. You can love a person and detest their belief system. Ask my roommate.

Plenty of people on the political right previously liked White House press secretary Scott McClellan, but now they wonder, *What's happened to this guy? Has he lost his mind?* No. He changed his beliefs; he didn't lose his mind. He's still the same intelligent, serious guy, and plenty "likable"—if you share his belief system.

As you can see, we base our belief systems on subjective interpretations. Now that you understand this, you can begin to benefit from the far-reaching implications of this insight.

To make this exercise work, force yourself to embrace people with different beliefs. Make yourself accept people who hold *radically* different beliefs from yours. Learn to separate the person from the person's belief system. You can now *decide* that you have never met a person you didn't like. It was the person's beliefs that you found offensive, distasteful, or dangerous, not the human being. Work on this exercise every day, just as you would do abs at the gym.

I initially learned this lesson from my friend Mother Teresa, and its value has been confirmed by my psychological research.

Like everyone.

It's a cornerstone of the Brain Mechanic cognitive exercises, and I guarantee it will change your life.

Pet Peeve Reversal

This is one of my favorite exercises, because it sums up the drive of this whole book. Make a list of twenty pet peeves.

Think hard.

The list might include restaurants, names, sounds, people, places, ideas, concepts, sayings, accents, songs, authors, television shows, movies, books, artists—the possibilities are endless. Just be sure they are things you despise. Choose pet peeves that the people closest to you could easily identify as your big gripes. Green peas. Old Western movies. Wet socks. Squeaky doors. Mispelings and tpyos. When people say "Three AM in the morning." You name it. What things do you really *loathe*.

Now, let's go back to what Darwin wrote: "In the struggle for survival, the fittest win out because they succeed in *adapting* themselves best to their environment" (my emphasis).

If we apply Darwin's principle of survival to psychology, we find he is saying something critical about our psychological survival.

Darwin says *change to survive*.

The cognitive model says *change to survive*.

Do I hear an echo? Not at all. The truth is: stagnation is not a viable option. So what beliefs have you changed? Have you changed any important ones? Have you changed anything meaningful? What beliefs have you changed recently? Today?

If you aren't changing, you aren't evolving; and if you aren't evolving, you're dying.

This exercise involves changing your pet peeves—*reversing* them, in fact. Yes, that's right: change five of your pet peeves from loathe to love. It doesn't matter which five you change, but decide to like them.

"What?" you exclaim incredulously.

That's right, you heard me. That song you always hated, that restaurant you "couldn't stand," the wallpaper your neighbor has, drinks served a certain way, and so on. From now on, *love* them all. The song you hated, play it. And don't roll your eyes.

Force yourself to find something lovable in the things you can't stand, and if you can't find anything, then force yourself to believe that persevering in this cognitive exercise will ultimately strengthen you, and love them anyway.

- Change your beliefs. Opinions are simply beliefs.
- Change your opinions. Change your tastes.
- Bend. Evolve. Survive. Stretch your brain.
- Changing an opinion is stretching your beliefs.

Your beliefs are the walls in your brain. Events and people and emotions bounce and reflect off of them. Tear down all the walls that keep reflecting unhealthy, negative stuff. Remodel the beliefs that are causing bad emotions. Take out a room, add a patio, put in double doors. You have control over your beliefs. Use that power to your advantage. This opens up a whole new universe of possibilities—you can believe *anything* you want to.

That's heavy. That's about as heavy as it gets.

Your beliefs are the house in your brain, and you can live in any kind of house you want to. Build yourself a custom cognitive retreat in your skull. Start changing today. Change your beliefs. Adapt or die.

PFC Yoga

Those of you who do yoga understand how beneficial stretching is to physical health. So when did you last put your prefrontal cortex through a killer yoga routine?

Stretch your beliefs just as gymnasts stretch their hamstrings. You're less likely to injure something that's been sufficiently stretched. Your brain is the same way. Stretch it.

Take a blank piece of paper and write down thirty of your big beliefs. Brainstorm and be creative. Talk to your family members or spouse to help you along. List some of your major beliefs.

Now, change *all* of them. That's my challenge for you. You don't need to change them all at once or forever, just give change a try. (I hear you Cubs fans; and the answer is, yes, you can also root for the Sox—if you *choose* to!) If your new beliefs don't enrich your life, change them again to something totally different. If those don't work, change them back.

By making a list and consciously working on changing your beliefs, you will engage the rational, conscious, reflective part of your brain, which will force your cingulate to switch out of the negative emotional cycle it's stuck in and allow you to gain rational perspective on the situation. Engineer your beliefs to suit your happiness and goals.

You may say, "Okay, I can do that, but the rational state doesn't last long. A few minutes later the old irrational beliefs creep back in, and the painful emotion returns." I understand precisely what you are saying, but I promise you it is better to spend all day squashing your irrational beliefs, even if they come back a thousand times, than to surrender to *irrationality*, and get swept away into a flood of painful emotions caused by your irrational beliefs.

Remember, cognitive therapy is a *highly active*, not a passive system. You must seriously work at it. It is your choice to think through emotional algebra and work at changing your beliefs, or to blank out and surrender to lizygdala.

Whenever you allow yourself to be swept away by an emotion, it is because you keep accepting and *reinforcing* your irrational belief. If you want to stop the flood of negative emotions, you must fight to replace the irrational belief with a rational belief, and short-circuit that cingulate loop.

Pop open your skull like a mechanic, put a leash on lizygdala, and go to work on your beliefs. Change, change, change. You're wrong about more than you think you're wrong about. Start changing your beliefs. Try some of the examples I provide below. You'll discover some things you believed to be true for you turn out to be false. It feels good to discover you are wrong—it means you're evolving.

Evolve. There's a giant new, fresh, exciting world waiting for you out there—but only you can choose to see it.

Florescent Funeral

For fifteen years I dressed in black as often as possible. I love black for all sorts of practical reasons: it doesn't show stains; it's easy to match; it's unobtrusive and slimming. Black clothing was my wardrobe staple. After learning the cognitive model and deciding to do some PFC Yoga of my own, I ran all over town buying brightly colored clothing. I started wearing vivid neon biking clothes that were sporty and bright. My wardrobe switched to Day-Glo, and I loved it. Something I used to make fun of, and thought I hated, I came to love.

We have a cultural belief system about black clothing— we wear it to funerals for "traditional" reasons, but life should not be lived like a funeral. If your fashion sense is conservative, mix it up and wear something offbeat and daring. If you normally shop at resale, like I do, surprise everyone by sporting something brand-new that you bought with the tags still on.

Personal fashion statements are expressions of your *opinion* about what looks good. Opinions are beliefs, so clothing is an easy place to start changing your beliefs, tastes, and traditions. Try mixing up your matchy-matchy black electronic devices with colorful ones. My new phone is neon pink—yikes! Nope—yum. You can believe anything you want about a pink phone or a neon orange laptop. Change your tastes—it's an excellent brain workout.

Big Green J

The next time a pang of jealousy sticks you in the gut, acknowledge the source (it's that little *gut* in your brain called your lizygdala) and decide immediately to change your belief about that relationship. Do it. It works. I promise you. If you feel jealousy that you've lost a man or woman to someone else, tell yourself that they need to be with this other person to realize and appreciate what they missed with you. Whether or not they ever do so is irrelevant; what matters is that you get some emotional relief. Jealousy is irrational and avoidable; just remember: you love who you believe you love.

If you are pining for someone who broke up with you, try sitting down with a pad of paper and making a list of all the current and foreseeable drawbacks to a relationship with that person. List everything—from the big stuff, like their drinking problem, moodiness, and lack of a job, to little things like chronic log sawing and remote hogging.

You now have control over emotions concerning your relationships, because you have control over your beliefs about your relationships. You know emotional algebra, so you know your beliefs about events and things will cause your emotions. Now you know *how*. Events alone cannot cause emotions; beliefs can. Your emotions are *your* responsibility, and now you have the tools to start working on them.

Longest Line Wins

There is a dangerous fallacy floating around regarding anger. Some people believe it is "conventional wisdom" that it's healthy to vent your anger; to "let it all out." It's vital for you to understand that there is not a shred of scientific evidence corroborating this notion. In fact, all the research about emotion shows that practice makes perfect. Experiments demonstrate that when people practice venting their anger—shouting, throwing tantrums, banging their fists on the table—their brains get more efficient at becoming angrier faster (and staying angrier longer). If you have anger issues, and you think letting it out is healthy, you're wrong. By "venting" your rage, you're actually rehearsing for your most destructive future explosions. The less you indulge each angry episode, the less angry you become overall. If you practice being angry long enough, you'll become perfect at it. Anger also causes microtears in blood vessels,

READER/CUSTOMER CARE SURVEY

HEFG

We care about your opinions! Please take a moment to fill out our online Reader Survey at **http://survey.hcibooks.com**.
As a **"THANK YOU"** you will receive a **VALUABLE INSTANT COUPON** towards future book purchases
as well as a **SPECIAL GIFT** available only online! Or, you may mail this card back to us.

(PLEASE PRINT IN ALL CAPS)

First Name _____ MI. _____ Last Name _____

Address _____ City _____

State _____ Zip _____ Email _____

1. Gender
□ Female □ Male

2. Age
□ 8 or younger
□ 9-12 □ 13-16
□ 17-20 □ 21-30
□ 31+

3. Did you receive this book as a gift?
□ Yes □ No

4. Annual Household Income
□ under $25,000
□ $25,000 - $34,999
□ $35,000 - $49,999
□ $50,000 - $74,999
□ over $75,000

5. What are the ages of the children living in your house?
□ 0 - 14 □ 15+

6. Marital Status
□ Single
□ Married
□ Divorced
□ Widowed

7. How did you find out about the book?
(please choose one)
□ Recommendation
□ Store Display
□ Online
□ Catalog/Mailing
□ Interview/Review

8. Where do you usually buy books?
(please choose one)
□ Bookstore
□ Online
□ Book Club/Mail Order
□ Price Club (Sam's Club, Costco's, etc.)
□ Retail Store (Target, Wal-Mart, etc.)

9. What subject do you enjoy reading about the most?
(please choose one)
□ Parenting/Family
□ Relationships
□ Recovery/Addictions
□ Health/Nutrition
□ Christianity
□ Spirituality/Inspiration
□ Business Self-help
□ Women's Issues
□ Sports

10. What attracts you most to a book?
(please choose one)
□ Title
□ Cover Design
□ Author
□ Content

TAPE IN MIDDLE; DO NOT STAPLE

|||| ||

BUSINESS REPLY MAIL
FIRST-CLASS MAIL PERMIT NO 45 DEERFIELD BEACH, FL

POSTAGE WILL BE PAID BY ADDRESSEE

Health Communications, Inc.
3201 SW 15th Street
Deerfield Beach FL 33442-9875

Comments

FOLD HERE

which over a period of decades can actually be deadly. Make no mistakes: Anger kills. The best way to eliminate it from your life is to nip it in the bud by changing your irrational beliefs before you get heated up. This exercise is a good example of how.

In the past, I'd make myself angry waiting in lines, but now I've turned the experience into a cognitive exercise. I use long lines at the grocery store and in traffic to stretch my PFC and change my beliefs. I believed that lines equaled delays, so I thought that the longer a line, the more of my time was being wasted. As long as I believed that lines were something negative like delays or a waste of time, I felt anger and annoyance upon encountering them. Now that I have chosen to believe that every line is an opportunity to strengthen my cognitive skills, I enjoy waiting in lines. I see them as happy opportunities.

The next time you're checking out at the supermarket, find the longest and slowest line, and get in it. Force yourself to believe that the longer you wait in that line, the better a cognitive workout you will have, and the stronger your cognitive skills will become. This exercise will teach you that you control your emotions when it comes to waiting in lines. Waiting is what you believe it is.

I can stand in a line for half an hour with a gentle smile. People in front and behind will huff and stomp and snort. I stand there with a smile because I have cognitive skills. I believe (when I need to) the longer the line, the better. You have never wasted time being patient.

Microevolution

Darwin was right. Adaptation is the key to survival. Evolution is simply change. If you are not changing, you are not evolving. Start making changes in your daily life, from large ones to small ones.

If you're a neat freak, leave a room messy for weeks. If you're a slob, keep one room *so* clean that your friends grow suspicious and ask you questions about what exactly you do in there. Watch the "Spouse-Swap" TV shows for a study in IB systems—people trapped in absolutistic beliefs in which neat/messy are considered morally right/wrong, rather than matters of preference, taste, and so on. These shows are excellent studies in *change*, and the subjects are usually better people for enduring the entire process.

If you're a minimalist, pack a whole room with knick-knacks and decorative items. If you love clutter, throw away everything but a chair and a table in one room. Do the opposite of what you normally do. Change. Stretch your brain. Stretch your PFC.

Never kept a blog on the computer? Start one. Been blogging for years? Pry yourself away from the keyboard and spend some time out in the real world. If you're a chronic text messenger, have a live conversation instead. Better yet, turn off your cell phone for a day, or even a week, and interact with everyone face-to-face. Write a paper letter and really freak someone out. If you only read fiction, read history. If you only read nonfiction, read a novel. Etc., etc., etc., etc.

Flex. Grow. Stretch. Experiment. Make yourself change.

Force yourself to make yourself change. *Force* yourself to make yourself force yourself to change.

Only watch Channel 5 news? Watch Channel 8. Only vacation on sandy beaches? Hit the icy tundra. Force yourself to microevolve every day by changing things you've become comfortable with. Get out of your comfort zone and try something new. It changes your brain. Changing your brain changes you.

What you change is not so important. *That* you change is vital. If you always sleep on one side of the bed, switch to the other side. Wear your watch on your right hand instead of your left. Change things. Change small things, and change big things. If you change something big, with frustrating consequences, change it back, or change it to something else. You're not making a lifelong commitment; you're experimenting with evolution, and you can take it.

Nature likes to select traits from big litters with lots of variations. Go wild with your experiments, and give your evolutionary process a lot of variation to choose from. And if you're already a chronic-change junkie, perhaps *change* for you is to *stop changing* for a while. If you're constantly fixing what isn't broken, change by stopping those unneeded fixes. Maybe *your* biggest change is staying the same for a while.

Pro-Cognitive Music

Your choice of music has a powerful cognitive influence on you. Choose songs that reinforce rational beliefs, not irrational beliefs. For instance, if you're going through a painful breakup, falling to pieces with Patsy Cline isn't a good cognitive choice. Try Journey's *I'll Be Alright Without You* or Gloria Gaynor's *I Will Survive.* Our conscious and subconscious thought processes, as well as our emotions, are deeply connected to music. Harness the power of song, and use it to strengthen your rational beliefs, and replace the irrational beliefs that cause painful emotions. I have a whole folder of songs in my iPod called Everything's Gonna Be All Right — it's my "pro-cog" folder.

Letting Go

This is an exercise I also call, "What to do when you don't know what to do." The answer is usually "let go." Becoming embroiled in a tense argument about religion or politics with someone? Let go of it. Feeling irate about the extra sixty cents they charged you at the $4.99 pizza buffet? Let go. Feel yourself clinging to an unrealistic self-image — those love handles, for example? Let go. And I'm not suggesting you let go forever. There is a time to stand your ground, and there's a time to concede it. Concede it when you need emotional relief from a possibly explosive situation. Remember the old adage "choose your battles wisely," and keep in mind that you have time to let go, regroup, and approach the situation again without the same surge of emotional intensity.

- Take a deep, fat tummy breath, and then let go of your belief.
- Let go of irrational thoughts. Let go of an argument. Let go of a win. Let go.
- Let go of that vicious cingulate cycle.
- Let go of lizygdala. Let go of must.

■ Let go of now. The only real *nows* are heart attacks, choking, and SOLs (ask your lawyer). Get rid of irrational *nows*, unless you're in the middle of a medical emergency or staring at a badge.

Umbrella Belief

This is an exercise that you can use in a hurry when you can't work through your emotional algebra, and you need help—*fast*.

Take a fat tummy breath, and then immediately believe that whatever event or challenge you have encountered is for the sole purpose of strengthening your cognitive skills. You may want to tell yourself that the more daunting the challenge, the more buff and impressive your cognitive muscles will be. Maybe you always wanted to be able to afford that fancy gym with the climbing wall, right? When life deals you really tough events, consider yourself lucky to finally afford a crack at that wall.

Make this your umbrella belief: "Anything disturbing or upsetting that comes my way is an opportunity to practice my new cog-skills." This umbrella belief has gotten me out of quite a few jams. You can always decide that any situation or circumstance is an *opportunity* for a hard-core brain work-out. Beliefs strengthen and protect you.

DIY Exercises

You know the cognitive model now, so make your own exercises. No one gave me any of these exercises; I just created all of them as I went along, and now that you know how emotional algebra works, you can do likewise. Once I understood the cognitive model, I designed these to get some relief in my own emotional life. I spent much of my life at sea on waves of emotion that I thought I had no control over, and after being adrift for so long, I created these exercises to target my own specific needs. There are an infinite number of exercises left to create, so Do It Yourself with the cognitive model. When you feel an emotional disturbance, use your emotional algebra skills to invent a creative exercise to help you change your irrational beliefs. Perhaps the exercises you create for yourself will be far more interesting and effective than the ones I created. Personalize your cognitive journey any way that works for you.

Target your specific emotional needs. You will change your life when you create the exact right exercises for yourself. I did it, and so can you.

Read Supreme Court *Beliefs*

Supreme Court justices decide complicated cases involving complex issues. Each justice can have a different *belief* about how a case should be decided, what the law means, and how it applies. Remember the other word we used for *belief*? That's right, the justices settle cases by writing out their *opinions*. Read their beliefs, I mean, opinions. Reading them will teach you a lot about beliefs.

I remember the first time I started reading the court's opinions. I would get to the end of the first opinion and be thoroughly convinced it was entirely correct. Then, by the end of the next opinion/belief, I would be completely convinced that *that one* was right, and so on, and so on. Then you get to dissents, and you become totally convinced of some completely new belief, in fact, a completely opposite belief you had been convinced of moments ago. My opinion bounced back and forth like a tennis ball in a vigorous match. What a great workout!

Each opinion is full of its own facts, and "truths," and each is very compelling, but is each one "right"? It's right depending on which justice you are, or on which side of the case you're invested. It's right depending on what belief system you were born with, or taught, or for any other reason you hold, or are paid to hold. You call it "right" if you believe it's right. Opinions are beliefs, and both are flexible. You can change them based on compelling evidence, or you can change them based on needs, or even whims.

Start reading Supreme Court opinions—the full opinions of every justice. Just Google *Supreme Court decisions.* You will learn a lot from lawyers about the flexibility of beliefs. Lawyers prove that beliefs are for hire. Advertisers prove that beliefs are for sale.

Forgiveness Workout

Always remember that forgiveness is not a feeling or emotion; it is a belief, which means you choose it. It's under your control and it is very, very powerful. You should never wait until you feel compelled to forgive anyone, because that time may not arrive. Since forgiveness is a decision, a finite action taken by your brain (and an actual, physical change in the shape of neurons in your brain), you don't even have to wait until you feel inclined to forgive; just *do* it.

That is to say, change the irrational belief: "I cannot forgive this person." You can forgive them. Choose to. The power of forgiveness has far-reaching, positive cognitive consequences. To forgive is to free yourself from the weight of numerous negative emotions. It also frees those you held accountable. If you carry the burden of feeling resentment and anger toward someone, you project a prison of guilt onto that person and turn yourself into the jailer.

We all know that jailers expend vast resources to keep prisoners locked up, and the jailer is always on the alert, in a highly stressful and emotionally disturbed state of mind. While the penal system is spending a fortune to contain and control the inmates, the inmates mostly just lie around watching television all day.

It's the same in your brain with resentments. You, as the condemning party, can be stewing and steaming and grinding your teeth, wasting all kinds of mental and emotional energy: that's your PFC kick-starting your amygdala and your cingulate getting in on the vicious cycle. The person you are angry with is probably going about his business, happy as a clam, sitting around watching television.

Make the conscious decision to forgive someone, and you will not only free yourself from multiple negative emotions, you will also free the object of your forgiveness. When they are no longer your prisoner, you no longer have to be their guard, and you can start to put your energies to better use. You're only holding yourself hostage.

Write down the names of the people you resent or condemn.

Try to think of people whom you might have difficulty forgiving and deliberately reverse that mind set by consciously *choosing* to forgive them. You know how emotional algebra works now. In the case of forgiveness, the event (EV) in the formula is the person or their action that caused the resentment, the variable is what you believe their action has "made" you feel, and EM represents the emotional relief you will get from changing your belief about the action that you haven't forgiven.

$$EV + x = EM$$

Plug in the variables and watch the magic happen. Free your enemies, and free yourself in the process. This is a great exercise to kick off your personal cognitive revolution. Do it. Choose forgiveness. Change your irrational beliefs about other people being wrong, evil, or unforgivable and release all your petty feuds and festering resentments. Forgiveness will become one of the greatest and most powerful rational beliefs in your brain and in your life.

L'Esprit de l'Escalier

You've spent hundreds if not thousands of hours engaged in it, but you may not know there's a name for it. *L'esprit de l'escalier* literally (kinda) translates to "stairway wit," but the best English equivalent is "what I wish I woulda said," and it just means thinking of the best retort after it's too late.

At some time or another, we all wished we had thought of the perfect thing to say during an encounter—only to come up with the perfect response after the window of opportunity has closed. *L'esprit de l'escalier*, however, more often happens after slamming down a phone, storming out of a restaurant, or leaving a job interview.

Now that you know what it's called and can relate it to your own experience, you'll recognize how much cognitive time and cognitive energy you waste in *l'esprit de l'escalier* Thinking back to our brain anatomy lesson, you know exactly where it leads. Yes—to the vicious cingulate cycle of the thought getting stuck in your brain and going around and around in circles until you can't even think about anything else—until you can't seem to let go of it.

I recently applied for a passport and found myself feeling frustrated and ruminating in my own *l'esprit de l'escalier*. The woman in the passport office drilled me with questions that caught me off guard by their personal nature. I spent almost two days afterward thinking back through her questions—hundreds of times—and coming up with clever comebacks I wish I *woulda said* to the woman. It was a waste of two whole days of cognitive energy.

If you ever get caught in a *l'esprit de l'escalier* cingulate cycle, remember the words of Omar Khayyam, an eleventh-century polymath, mathematician, philosopher, astronomer, physician, and poet:

> The Moving Finger writes, and having writ,
> Moves on: nor all your Piety nor Wit
> Shall lure it back to cancel half a line,
> Nor all your tears wash out a Word of it.

> —71, The Rubaiyat of Omar Khayyam

Don't waste any time or unnecessary energy stressing out over what you wish you would've said. Use the cognitive model to replace your irrational beliefs about what you *shoulda said* in an encounter with rational ones. Initially, with the woman at the passport office, I thought, *She thinks I'm lying or trying to pull some kind of fast one! I'm an American, and this is my own government talking to me like I'm a stranger! Her office exists to serve U.S. citizens, so she shouldn't act like I'm on trial here! She must treat me differently!* But finally I put my crystal ball exercise to work. I imagined this: What if I take off on another long trip into the uncharted islands of Indonesia, or the rarely toured eastern states of India . . . and, bang! I catch a case of dengue fever. And what if I hadn't told anyone how far I was traveling and I couldn't find a phone, and my condition became life-threatening? Aha! All those personal questions she asked me, like "What countries have you visited . . . are you planning to go anywhere soon?" will still exist in my file, and someone will open the file and extrapolate (from all the personal questions she asked me) where I might be, and contact the right embassies, and secure transport and medical care. Of course, it's highly unlikely any of her questions or my answers will ever matter. But I convinced myself that there is the possibility that all those questions could one day result in my own benefit, rather than viewing them as an invasion of my privacy. Omar Khayyam nailed this one. Avoid *l'esprit de l'escalier* cingulate cycles, and move on. Let go, and move on.

Being Immortally Challenged

Oh, there is a *must* I forgot to mention. Someday you're going to kick your oxygen habit. Like it or not, it's beyond your control. No one here gets out alive. But guess what? You can believe anything you want to about death—your own, and anyone else's. There are thousands of options here. You have to live your own life and die your own death, so you might as well believe something constructive about the whole business. The main thing you can control regarding death is your belief about it.

You can believe whatever you want—that when you pass on you'll be sleeping with the fishes, or singing with the angels. Be creative with this one. It's the only real way out.

Stay Abreast of Cognitive Research!

I cannot stress this one enough: set up News Alerts in your favorite Internet clearinghouse. Go to Google News, and follow the links to personalize your news page. Most news sites offer this feature. Enter these as news-search keywords: "cognitive behavioral therapy," "cognition," "prefrontal cortex," and so on, and your news page will suggest articles for you to read on these topics. Now that you know a little more about *how* your brain works, collect and study all the latest research from the frontiers of the cognitive revolution. There are tens of thousands of pages about CBT online. Explore the research. Every day new studies reveal the power of CBT.

Take my word for it. You'll be shocked by how much you'll understand the literature and articles you read. You have a fantastic edge because you have a functional knowledge of the cognitive model based on what you've learned here.

CBT is real. It's testable. It's powerful. It WORKS.

This can work for anyone, and you can use it now. You know the basics. You can harness its power. CBT is the most powerful evidence-based tool available to psychotherapists and available to you free as your own Brain Mechanic. Read all you can about it. Reap the rewards.

Part

Four

THE BRAIN MECHANIC ACTION PLAN:

Five Quick Steps to
Emotional Well-being

Now that you've tested your Brain Mechanic tools — by way of these exercises — you have the power to experience the life-altering benefits of CBT. The following five-step action plan synthesizes the basics of our Brain Mechanic journey into survival psychology.

If you learn this one action plan, I promise it will change your life for the better, forever.

The instant you feel an emotional disturbance (anger, disappointment, stress, anxiety):

1) **IMMEDIATELY** take a deep, **fat tummy breath.**

2) **Stop Boomerangs.** Accept the original signal from your lizygdala. Whatever emotion you just felt is okay. Tell yourself (or, if it helps, say it aloud): "This surge of rage/adrenaline/fear — it's just my lizygdala helping me survive. I accept this emotion, but now it's cognitive time . . ." This acceptance prevents the cingulate from getting stuck in a self-reinforcing loop of Boomerang Emotions.

3) **Locate the thought (that is, the irrational belief).** Ask yourself, "What was I thinking the instant I felt that emotion?" Identification is key.

4) **Look for the *must*.** If you felt anger or rage, look for a *must* assumption that you are making about other people. If you felt anxiety or panic, look for a *must* assumption about yourself. Locate the irrational belief (IB) (or *must*) that caused the emotion (EM).

5) **Squash the irrational belief** that is causing your emotional disturbance. Replace this irrational belief (IB) with an alternate, rational belief, and fire away with machine-gun rational thoughts. Make your personalized list of machine-gun rational statements (see page 66) and memorize it.

Practicing the Brain Mechanic techniques will actually transform the structures in your brain, help you escape emotional disturbances, and improve your mood, your relationships, and your communication skills.

Memorize these action steps; they will change your life:

1) Take a fat tummy breath.
2) Accept emotion.
3) Locate the irrational belief.
4) Remove the *must*.
5) Change the irrational belief to a rational one.

POP QUIZ: *What is the first thing you do when something disturbs you?*

> **Breathe.** That's right. Fat tummy breath. Breathe first, then accept the emotion (EM), locate the irrational belief (IB), remove the *must*, and, finally, change your irrational belief (IB) to a rational one (RB).

Write the action steps on an index card and carry it in your wallet, or post the card throughout the house and in the car.

If you learn and practice these five steps in the order shown above, you will be able to fix any emotional flat tire you encounter along the bumpy road of life. You are your own Brain Mechanic. You possess the tools of survival psychology, and your journey to emotional freedom has just begun.

* * *

"Live your beliefs and you can
turn the world around."

—HENRY DAVID THOREAU

Grand Unification

Science and faith coexist in the Brain Mechanic cognitive model. Nothing in this book requires that you relinquish your rational mind. "Faith" can exist separately from religion and mysticism for completely rational reasons.

All my life I heard people say, "Believe! You only have to believe!" But you might as well have handed me a brick and a stick and said, "Push! You only have to push!"

Um, push what? Push? Where? I don't know *how*. I need a diagram! I needed someone to show me how to position the brick (like a fulcrum), and where to put the stick, and how and where to push. *Someone needs to give me the picture.*

"Believe!" is as meaningless as "Push!" if you don't have a diagram. The cognitive model shows you how your emotions (EMs) work and gives your beliefs context, meaning, and functional power. The cognitive model teaches the religious or spiritually minded naturalists how to use their faith.

As a scientist, my faith isn't supernatural, nor is it related to "spiritualism" of any kind. My faith is my own power to alter my brain physically in ways that enhance my life and help move me toward my goals. These tools can be used quite effectively as well in conjunction with anyone's specific religious or spiritual beliefs. No one had ever explained to me the many ways in which events (EVs), thoughts, and emotions (EMs) are connected by beliefs (Bs). And no one ever told me I could be a die-hard überskeptic and have plenty of room left for being a *believer*.

To summarize, you're not an idiot; you probably just got incomplete instructions. You always knew *what* to do and *why* to do it, but perhaps didn't know HOW. But now— with emotional algebra and flexible beliefs—you know precisely how. You have the power to adapt, evolve, survive, and thrive as one of the psychologically fittest.

My discovery brings together the sometimes opposing views of science, psychology, and faith. The Brain Mechanic cognitive model has changed my life for the better, and I'm grateful that you gave me the chance to share it with you. You have all the basic tools needed to roll up your sleeves and go to work on your brain. This is only the beginning of your cognitive journey, but you are already your own Brain Mechanic.

I will leave you with a directive that I used to loathe because I didn't understand, but now I love—because I *changed*:

Believe.

You are now post-cognitive.

Welcome to the Revolution . . .

Acknowledgments

My love and gratitude to my parents, especially my mom, Joy, whose years of clinical psychotherapeutic work with high-risk youth have been an invaluable resource in creating the cognitive exercises presented in this book.

Profound thanks to Mother Teresa, M.C. Without her friendship and guidance this book would not exist. Very special thanks to David Geffen for his patience and friendship. A heartfelt thank-you to Dr. Cheryl Saban, without whom I couldn't have done it. Thank you to Mark Abrams and Jayne Friedman for their comments, reflections, and critiques. Special thanks to Sheri Salata for her kind attention. Special thanks to my editor Michele Matrisciani, and Ann Gossy and Candace Johnson for their guidance, patience, and linguistic genius. Warmest gratitude to my *Townhouse* friends: Princess Carole Radziwill, Lori Andrews, Bruce Vilanch, Christopher Ciccone, Prince Manvendra Singh Gohil, Belinda Mason, and Gisela Getty.

I am indebted to the University of Chicago, especially my

teachers and friends: John Kehlen, Nathan Tarcov, Jamie Redfield, Mortimer Adler, Jim McCawley, and others. Thanks to Allan Bloom for knowledge and friendship and to Scott Klein for believing in my mind.

Thank you Dr. Elizabeth-Anne Stewart, Stacey Spain, Esq., Marc Aguila, Michael Kutza, Richard Sorman Esq., Dr. Cole, and Dr. Freddie Shick for years of friendship. Thank you, Dr. Richard Dowling for the music and Gordon Sinclair for the food.

I am enormously grateful to Arianna Huffington, Steve and Janet Wozniak, Carole Bayer Sager, Elayne Boosler, Art Smith and Jesus Salguerio, Sean Lewis, Jesse Brune, Michael Butler, Meghan Stabler, Betty Buckley, Gerald and Trisha Posner, Mario Cantone, Hilary Rosen, Joe Zuniga, Howard Bragman, Jim Grissom, Edie McClurg, Gerald and Trisha Posner, Maria Dorfner, Corey Spears, Greg Archer, and ANT for their support and encouragement.

Special thanks to my agent, Felicia Eth, for patience and endurance. Thank you, Donnie Young, Etienne Padin, Melinda Herron, Greg Jarvis, Dr. Amin Ghaziani, Angela Jordan, Scott Casty, Adrian Casadas, Bill Haddad, Tim Weber, Mike O'Hara, Jay Deratany, Anneke Sterling, Stu Zirin, Gus Atsalis, and Billy Candelario for the history. Thank you, Carlos and Elizabeth Fielding Oropeza for Paradise House, and Michael Thompson for the White House. Thanks to Epictetus, who started all this, and Auntie Mame, who gave it jewelry. Thank you, Rhonda Noonan, M.S., L.P.C., clinical director, and Dr. Jack Apsche at the Apsche Clinic.

I am deeply indebted to Dr. Aaron Beck, Dr. Albert Ellis,

Dr. Daniel Amen, Dr. Eric Berne, and Dr. David Burns for their pioneering work. Thanks to the Newberry Library for giving me 14,000 books, and Public Storage for letting me operate my library therein.

Thanks to Ambassador Wong Cheeks Tahiti for the deep-limbic therapy of warm fur and a cold nose. Thanks to my solitude—in which I do my best work. Thanks to the great City of Chicago for being so cold, and the United States of America for being so warm.

Deepest gratitude to everyone who reads this book—you're the reason I wrote it. I'm grateful that you gave me the most precious thing you have—your time.

Finally, eternal thanks to the coterie of geeky ghosts who haunt my every waking hour: Ron Propp, Frank Casey, Billy Dose, Allan Bloom, Dr. Randolph Tucker, Charles Darwin, and Harry Mencken.

Bibliography

Adler, A. (1929) *The science of living*. New York: Greenberg.

Adler, A. (1931) *What life should mean to you*. New York: Blue Ribbon Books.

Amen, D. G. (1999) *Change your brain, change your life: The breakthrough program for conquering anxiety, depression, obsessiveness, anger, and impulsiveness*. New York: Three Rivers Press.

Amen, D. G. (2008) *Healing the hardware of the soul: Enhance your brain to improve your work, love, and spiritual life*. New York: Free Press.

Amen, D. G. (2008) *Magnificent mind at any age: Natural ways to unleash your brain's maximum potential*. New York: Harmony Books.

Atkinson, B. J. (2005) *Emotional intelligence in couples therapy: Advances from neurobiology and the science of intimate relationships*. New York: W. W. Norton.

Beck, A. T. (1976) *Cognitive therapy and the emotional disorders*. New York: International Universities Press.

Beck, A. T. (1988) *Love is never enough: How couples can*

overcome misunderstandings, resolve conflicts, and solve relationship problems through cognitive therapy. New York: Harper & Row.

Beck, A. T. (1999) *Prisoners of hate: The cognitive basis of anger, hostility, and violence.* New York: HarperCollins.

Berne, E. (1964) *Games people play: The basic handbook of transactional analysis.* New York: Ballantine Books.

Burns, D. D. (1980) *Feeling good: The new mood therapy.* New York: Morrow.

Dryden, W. (1984) *Rational-emotive therapy.* In W. Dryden, *Individual therapy in Britain* (pp. 235–63). London: Harper & Row.

Dryden, W., & Golden, W. L. (1986) *Cognitive-behavioral approaches to psychotherapy.* London: Harper & Row.

Ellis, A. (1957) *How to live with a neurotic: At home and at work.* New York: Crown. Revised edition, Hollywood, CA: Wilshire Books, 1975.

Ellis, A. (1973) *Humanistic psychotherapy: The rational-emotive approach.* New York: McGraw-Hill.

Ellis, A. (1977) *Anger—how to live with and without it.* Secaucus, NJ: Citadel Press.

Ellis, A. (1985) *Overcoming resistance: Rational-emotive therapy with difficult clients.* New York: Springer.

Ellis, A. (1998) *How to control your anxiety before it controls you.* New York: Citadel Press.

Ellis, A. (1999) *How to make yourself happy and remarkably less disturbable.* Atascadero, CA: Impact Publishers.

Ellis, A. (2001) *Overcoming destructive beliefs, feelings, and behaviors: New directions for rational emotive behavior therapy.* New York: Prometheus Books.

Ellis, A., & Dryden, W. (1987) *The practice of rational-emotive therapy.* New York: Springer.

Ellis, A., & Harper, R. A. (1961) *A guide to rational living.* Englewood, CA: Prentice Hall.

Ellis, A., Lange, A. (1994) How to keep people from pushing your buttons. New York: Citadel Press.

Ellis, A., Wolfe, J. L., & Moseley, S. (1966) *How to raise an emotionally healthy, happy child.* North Hollywood, CA: Wilshire Books.

Epictetus. (1908) *The collected works of Epictetus.* Boston: Little, Brown.

Fenichel, O. (1945) *Psychoanalytic theory of neurosis.* New York: Norton.

Fisher, R. (2002) *Experiential psychotherapy with couples: A guide for the creative pragmatist.* Phoenix, AZ: Zeig, Tucker, and Theisen, Inc.

Frankl, V. (1959) *Man's search for meaning.* New York: Pocket Books.

Freud, S. (1905) *The interpretation of dreams.* London: Hogarth Press.

Freud, S. (1937) *The ego and the mechanisms of defense.* London: Hogarth.

Freud, S. (1965) *Standard edition of the complete psychological works of Sigmund Freud.* London: Hogarth.

Gazzaniga, M. S. (2006) *The ethical brain: The science of our moral dilemmas.* New York: Harper Perennial.

Gazzaniga, M. S. (2008) *Cognitive neuroscience: The biology of the mind.* New York: W. W. Norton.

Gazzaniga, M. S. (2008) *Human: The science behind what makes your brain unique.* New York: HarperCollins.

Glasser, W. (1965) *Reality Therapy.* New York: Harper & Row.

Goldfried, M. R., & Merbaum, M. (1973) *Behavior change through self-control.* New York: Holt, Rinehart & Winston.

Goleman, D. (1995) *Emotional intelligence.* New York: Bantam.

Goleman, D. (2000) *Working with emotional intelligence.* New York: Bantam.

Grieger, R., & Grieger, I. (1982) *Cognition and emotional disturbance.* New York: Human Sciences Press.

Guidano, V. F., & Liotti, G. (1983) *Cognitive processes and emotional disorders.* New York: Guilford.

Heidegger, M. (1962) *Being and time.* New York: Harper & Row.

Hoffer, E. (1951) *The true believer.* New York: Harper & Row.

Horney, K. (1945) *Our inner conflicts.* New York: Norton.

Horney, K. (1950) *Neurosis and human growth.* New York: Norton.

Janis, I. L. (1983) *Short-term counseling.* New Haven, CT: Yale University Press.

Kendall, P. C., & Braswell, L. (1984) *Cognitive behavioral therapy for impulsive children.* New York: Guilford.

Knaster, M. (1996) *Discovering the body's wisdom: A comprehensive guide to more than fifty mind-body practices that can relieve pain, reduce stress, and foster health, spiritual growth, and inner peace.* New York: Bantam Books.

Krueger, D. W. (1989) *Body self and psychological self: A developmental and clinical integration of disorders of the self.* New York: Brunner/Mazel.

Kuhn, T. S. (1970) *The structure of scientific revolutions* (2nd ed.). Chicago: University of Chicago Press.

Lazarus, A. A. (1971) *Behavior therapy and beyond*. New York: McGraw-Hill.

Lazarus, A. A. (1981) *The practice of multimodal therapy*. New York: McGraw-Hill.

LeDoux, J. (1998) *The emotional brain: The mysterious underpinnings of emotional life*. New York: Touchstone Books.

Mahoney, M. J. (1974) *Cognition and behavior modification*. Cambridge, MA: Ballinger.

Martin, J. (1987) *Cognitive-instructional counseling*. Canada: Althouse Press.

Maslow, A. H. (1954) *Motivation and personality*. New York: Harper & Row.

Maultsby, M. C., Jr. (1984) *Rational behavior therapy*. Englewood Cliffs, NJ: Prentice Hall.

McMullin, R. (1986) *Handbook of cognitive therapy techniques*. New York: Norton.

Medina, J. J. (2008) *12 principles for surviving and thriving at work, home, and school*. Seattle, WA: Pear Press.

Meichenbaum, D. (1977) *Cognitive-behavioral modification*. New York: Plenum.

Pavlov, I. (1927) *Conditioned reflexes*. New York: Liverlight.

Perls, F. (1969) *Gestalt therapy verbatim*. Lafayette, CA: Real People Press.

Popper, K. R. (1963) *Conjectures and refutations*. New York: Harper & Bros.

Reichenbach, H. (1953) *The rise of scientific philosophy*. Berkeley: University of California Press.

Rogers, C. R. (1961) *On becoming a person*. Boston: Houghton-Mifflin.

Russell, B. (1965) *The basic writings of Bertrand Russell*. New York: Simon & Schuster.

Saban, C. (2010) *What is your self-worth? A woman's guide to validation*. London: Hay House.

Seligman, M. (1975) *Helplessness*. San Francisco: Freeman.

Skinner, B. F. (1971) *Beyond freedom and dignity*. New York: Knopf.

Tavris, C. (1983) *Anger: The misunderstood emotion*. New York: Simon & Schuster.

Walen, S. R., DiGiuseppe, R. A., & Wessler, R. L. (1980) *A practitioner's guide to rational-emotive therapy*. New York: Oxford Press.

Walter, J. L., & Peller, J. E. (1992) *Becoming solution-focused in brief therapy*. New York: Brunner/Mazel.

Watzlawick, P. (1984) *The invented reality: How do we know what we really know? Contributions to constructivism*. New York: Norton.

Wolpe, J. (1958) *Psychotherapy by reciprocal inhibition*. Stanford, CA: Stanford University Press.

Wolpe, J. (1982) *The practice of behavior therapy* (3rd ed.) New York: Pergamon Press.

Zilbergeld, B., & Lazarus, A. A. (1987) *Mind power*. Boston: Little, Brown.

Further Reading

I cannot overstate the importance of these authors and the work they have contributed to psychology and society. Every one of these books is a fantastic world of its own. Enjoy:

Archetypes of the Collective Unconscious, The by Carl Jung (Princeton University Press, 1981)

Authentic Happiness by Martin Seligman (Free Press, 2004)

Beyond Freedom and Dignity by B. F. Skinner (Hackett, 2002)

Blank Slate, The by Steven Pinker (Penguin, 2003)

Brain That Changes Itself, The by Norman Doidge (Penguin, 2007)

Brain Rules by John J. Medina (Pear Press, 2009)

Brain Sex by Anne Moir & David Jessel (Delta, 1992)

Change Your Brain Change Your Life by Daniel Amen (Three Rivers Press, 1999)

Conditioned Reflexes by Ivan Pavlov (Dover Publications, 2003)

Creativity by Mihaly Csikszentmihalyi (Harper Perennial, 1997)

Dimensions of Personality by Hans Eysenck (Transactions 1997)

Ego and the Mechanisms of Defense, The by Anna Freud (International Universities Press, 1982)

Emotional Intelligence by Daniel Goleman (Bantam, 2006)

Ethical Brain, The by Michael Gazzaniga (Dana Press, 2005)

Farther Reaches of Human Nature, The by Abraham Maslow (Penguin, 1993)

Feeling Good by David D. Burns (Harper, 1999)

Flow by Mihaly Csikszentmihalyi (Harper Perennial, 2008)

Games People Play by Eric Berne (Ballantine Books, 1999)

Gestalt Therapy by Frederick Perls (Gestalt Journal Press, 1977)

Getting to YES by Roger Fisher (Penguin, 1991)

Gift of Fear, The by Gavin de Becker (Dell, 1999)

Gifts Differing by Isabel Briggs Myers (Davies-Black, 1995)

Guide to Rational Living by Albert Ellis & Robert Harper (Wilshire Book Company, 1975)

How We Decide by Jonah Lehrer (Mariner Books, 2010)

I'm OK—You're OK by Thomas A. Harris (Galahad Books, 2004)

Influence by Robert Cialdini (Harper Paperbacks, 2006)

Interpretation of Dreams, The by Sigmund Freud (Basic Books, 2010)

Language and Thought of the Child, The by Jean Piaget (Goldberg Press, 2008)

Lateral Thinking by Edward de Bono (Harper Colophon, 1973)

Man's Search for Meaning by Viktor Frankl (Beacon Press, 2006)

Man Who Mistook His Wife for a Hat, The by Oliver Sacks (Touchstone, 1998)

On Becoming a Person by Carl Rogers (Mariner Books, 1995)

Paradox of Choice, The by Barry Schwartz (Harper Perennial, 2005)

People Skills by Robert Bolton (Touchstone, 1986)

Predictably Irrational by Dan Ariely (Harper Perennial, 2010)

Principles of Psychology, The by William James (Cosimo Classics, 2007)

Sociopath Next Door, The by Martha Stout (Broadway, 2006)

Stuff of Thought, The by Steven Pinker (Penguin, 2008)

Stumbling on Happiness by Daniel Gilbert (Vintage, 2007)

7 Principles for Making Marriage Work, The by John Gottman (Three Rivers Press, 2000)

Traffic by Tom Vanderbilt (Vintage 2009)

True Believer, The by Eric Hoffer (Harper Perennial, 2002)

Understanding Human Nature by Alfred Adler (Oneworld Publications, 2009)

Working with Emotional Intelligence by Daniel Goleman (Bantam, 2000)

Young Man Luther by Erik Erikson (W. W. Norton, 1993)

Index

About the Author

Spencer Lord traveled throughout Asia, teaching ESL and working for Mother Teresa in Calcutta, India, before his interest was sparked in cognitive psychology. Through writing, lecturing, and private consulting, he continues to pursue his passion of teaching creative-thought exercises based on the principles of cognitive behavioral therapy. He currently lives in Los Angeles, California, and India. Visit the author at www.thebrainmechanicbook.com.